CITY CENTRE CAMPUS
LEARNING & SKILLS CENTRE

You can renew your books b...

Emai...

D1348970

In Shakespeare's Playhouse

A
MIDSUMMER NIGHT'S
DREAM

In Shakespeare's Playhouse

THE POET'S METHOD
MACBETH
HAMLET
A MIDSUMMER NIGHT'S DREAM

Other volumes are in preparation

Maurice Percival

IN SHAKESPEARE'S PLAYHOUSE

BY
RONALD WATKINS
AND
JEREMY LEMMON

A MIDSUMMER NIGHT'S DREAM

DAVID & CHARLES

NEWTON ABBOT . LONDON . VANCOUVER

0 7153 6464 2

© Ronald Watkins and Jeremy Lemmon 1974

Set in 11pt on 13pt Aldine Bembo and printed
in Great Britain by Latimer Trend & Company
Ltd Plymouth for David & Charles (Holdings)
Limited South Devon House Newton Abbot
Devon

Published in Canada by Douglas David &
Charles Limited 3645 McKechnie Drive West
Vancouver BC

CONTENTS

PREFATORY NOTE   9

INTRODUCTION   11

A MIDSUMMER NIGHT'S DREAM   31

NOTES   144

PREFATORY NOTE

In this reconstruction of Shakespeare's play we have aimed to preserve a sense of the continuity of performance. It is important that the text of the play itself should be kept constantly in mind: quotations from the episode under discussion are printed in **bold type**; quotations from other parts of the play, and from other plays or books, have been placed inside inverted commas. In the quotations we have made as little departure from the lineation and punctuation of the early texts as has seemed compatible with the convenience of a modern reader; spelling, however, has been modernised. We have quoted stage-directions only from the Quartos and First Folio, since these, in most cases, may reasonably be supposed to reflect the practice of performance in Shakespeare's own playhouse; they are printed as they appear in the early texts, in italics, and not modernised in any way (except that we have abandoned the long 's', and the 'i' and 'u' which represent, respectively, 'j' and 'v').

For those readers who wish to keep Shakespeare's text by them as they read, we have added in the margin Act, Scene and Line numbers, as milestones of the play's progress. Since no universally standardised system of reference-numbering is yet conveniently available, we have chosen in these and other reference-numbers to follow the *Oxford Standard Authors* edition of Shakespeare's Works (edited by W. J. Craig), except when, for a particular purpose, another edition is specified.

Superior figures in the course of the commentary refer to the Notes which are grouped together at the end of the book.

INTRODUCTION

The aim of the present series is to reconstruct in imagination the performance of Shakespeare's plays in his own lifetime, and thereby
to throw the clearest possible light upon their overall design and the
minute detail of their writing. It is generally agreed that A MIDSUMMER
NIGHT'S DREAM was originally composed for a wedding-occasion.
Dover Wilson in his note on the copy (*New Cambridge* edition, 100)
postulates more than one marriage-celebration and suggests that the
play was 'first handled by Shakespeare in 1592 or before, rehandled in
1594, and rehandled once again in 1598'. Yet before 1600 it was being
performed in the public playhouse. For the title-page of the Quarto
text printed by Thomas Fisher in that year, presents the play 'as it hath
been sundry times publickely acted, by the Right honourable, the
Lord Chamberlaine his servants'. It is a public performance on one of
these 'sundry times' that we seek to reproduce.

The Fisher Quarto was printed from Shakespeare's manuscript (it is
included in the list of plays 'printed directly from foul papers' in
Charlton Hinman's Introduction to the Norton Facsimile, xv), and we
use its words as the basic authority for our reconstruction, working
also from the Folio text of 1623, which has some interesting variations,
especially in the stage-directions, and no doubt sometimes represents
stage-practice of a later date than 1600, practice which was familiar
however to Shakespeare's surviving fellow-actors, Heminges and
Condell. Dover Wilson's largely convincing analysis of the transmission of the text is marred by one strangely improbable implication,
that in Shakespeare's final version, as represented by Fisher's printing
of his foul papers, there survived a great deal of inferior material,
chiefly in the scenes involving the lovers. There are, he says, 'at least

two textual layers . . . one, represented chiefly by the dialogue of the lovers, which was written on the threshold of Shakespeare's career' (this 'layer' he considers to be crude in psychology and stiff in versification) 'and the other . . . which was written later' (and contains all the finest passages). In *Shakespeare's Happy Comedies* Dover Wilson went farther still and argued that A MIDSUMMER NIGHT'S DREAM was only partly by Shakespeare. His opinion suggests a curious conception of the processes of the playwright's craft and takes a somewhat pedagogic view—*de haut en bas*—of Shakespeare's composition at the ripe age of twenty-eight.

We assume, on the contrary, that whatever the process of evolution and revision, Shakespeare was content with the final draft in its entirety, and that whatever earlier material he kept in his final draft satisfied him as a congruous part of the whole. It seems to us moreover that the suggestion that the play was from time to time altered to suit a particular private occasion may contain only half the truth. It may well be argued that the final draft (the copy for the Fisher Quarto) reflects some adaptation for those public performances specified on the title-page, and includes some necessary expansion and broadening of interest to transform the esoteric and ephemeral appeal of a private occasion to the wider range of tastes needed to satisfy an audience in the public playhouse. Some such adaptation, we shall suggest, is centred especially upon the role of Theseus in the fifth Act of the play, enlarged and enriched in such a way as to present him as an enlightened patron of the arts, and to knit the whole Act, and indeed the whole play, into a coherent harmony.

The principles upon which our attempted reconstructions proceed are set forth in our Introductory Volume, but we append a brief recapitulation to prepare the reader for a visit to A MIDSUMMER NIGHT'S DREAM as presented in the public playhouse—the Theatre or the Curtain?—in the daylight of a London afternoon in the last years of the sixteenth century. We ask him to bear in mind certain known facts about the circumstances of Shakespeare's working life, and some conclusions which may be drawn from them:

(1) During most of the period when he was writing his plays,

Shakespeare was an active member of the most successful players' company in London; certainly at the time of the performance of A MIDSUMMER NIGHT'S DREAM which we seek to reconstruct, he was present at, and presumably taking a personal part in, the preparation and rehearsal of his plays.

(2) The plays were written to be performed by the regular members of the company which was established as the Chamberlain's Men in 1594, and it was soon after this date (so most scholars believe) that A MIDSUMMER NIGHT'S DREAM reached the public stage. T. W. Baldwin (*The Organization and Personnel of the Shakespearean Company*, 197, 303) has said of Shakespeare's creative method that 'the play was regularly fitted to the company, not the company to the play' and that his plays 'represent not only his own individual invention but also the collective invention of his company'. A MIDSUMMER NIGHT'S DREAM, involving the King and Queen of the Fairies and their separate 'trains' of attendants, made unusual demands of casting among the professionals of the company and entailed special recruiting of auxiliary players.

(3) The plays were presented in repertory—six different plays, by various authors, in a week—repeated at intervals only as long as they were successful in drawing an audience. These conditions preclude the idea of a director's designing and dressing a play as for a long run; but the special needs of creating the illusion of the fairy-haunted wood near Athens taxed the ingenuity of the company's wardrobe-managers beyond their normal resources.

(4) The company was extremely adaptable in performance; it was accustomed to appear at court or on tour, as well as in the playhouse. The possibility that A MIDSUMMER NIGHT'S DREAM was designed for a particular occasion suggests that the play was readily adaptable to accidental circumstances. Nevertheless we know that it found its way ultimately to the public playhouse, and it is probable that this, like most of Shakespeare's plays, was conceived in terms of this milieu, the daily setting of his working life; we may therefore assume that the physical and atmospheric conditions of performance in the public playhouse were constantly in his mind as he composed.

(5) Shakespeare's public playhouse was octagonal, polygonal or

circular, small but capacious, and open to the skies. We do not know its precise dimensions, but we can guess that the overall diameter was less than 100 feet, possibly as little as 80 feet; and that the diameter of the interior (with which we are chiefly concerned) was considerably less than the 78 feet which is the length of a lawn-tennis court. Yet its capacity was more than 2,000. The performance therefore could touch the extremes of intimacy and public address: the benighted Hermia, the foot-sore messenger Puck, Bottom awaking from his nightmare—all are momentarily alone, confiding their thoughts to each individual hearer in the auditorium; by contrast, the revels of the wedding-night are a public occasion at which the whole play-house audience warms its hands round the Duke's unseasonable midsummer fire.

(6) The great Stage projected into the audience, which stood or sat on three sides of it. The middle of the front of the Stage was the central point of the whole building. The background of the Stage was formed by the façade of the Tiring-House, behind which the actors attired themselves: in it were set two Doors, one on either side, through which the actors emerged on to the Stage. For much of the time the Stage was treated as independent of this background, and indeed the main span of A MIDSUMMER NIGHT'S DREAM, the long night in the wood, takes place *in vacuo*, geographically related for a time to the moss-bank on which Titania sleeps and the adjacent 'hawthorn brake' behind which Bottom is translated, but at other times unlocalised, so that the mind's eye of the audience, prompted by the words which the poet has put into the mouth of his players, receives other pictures: the pranks of 'that shrewd and knavish sprite, Call'd Robin Good-fellow', or the 'fair Vestal, throned by the West', or Helena's picture of 'schooldays friendship, childhood innocence. . . . Both on one sampler, sitting on one cushion', or Oberon's proud picture of how '. . . the Eastern gate all fiery red, Opening on Neptune, with fair blessed beams, Turns into yellow gold, his salt green streams'. It is this freedom from precise locality which presents to the actors the opportunity to give 'to airy nothing, A local habitation, and a name'.

(7) The Tiring-House, though the details of its architecture are

uncertain, was a permanent feature of the playhouse, familiar and accepted by the audience every time they came to the play. It could therefore be ignored altogether or, if such was the dramatist's wish, its features could be used, described and embodied in the action. In this play, since the action is largely out of doors, the Tiring-House can play little part in clarifying the narrative. A suggestion that the mechanicals had their home-base on the upper level from which they descended to the Stage for their rehearsal in the wood and their performance at court is no more than conjecture: but such a disposition would have had its theatrical purpose.* In the last Act the blessing of the house gained perhaps some added verisimilitude, if the Duke and Duchess appeared on the upper level on their way to bed, and Oberon and Titania followed them with their ritual of purgation: the Tiring-House with its gallery and Doors and the open Stage before it could suggest the interior of an Elizabethan great house. But the detachment of Stage from Tiring-House is nowhere so plainly evidenced as in the Fisher Quarto's unabashed description (echoed in the Folio) of the first appearance in the forest of the Fairy court: *Enter the King of Fairies, at one doore, with his traine; and the Queene, at another, with hers.*

(8)   Because of the proportions of Stage and auditorium, by which an actor could stand at the very central point of the whole playhouse, the audience were not detached spectators of a remote picture but engaged participants, often partisans, on the fringe of a live action taking place in their midst. Thus the cross-stage wrangle of the Fairy court is reinforced by a claque of groundlings on either side of the Yard; the lovers in their lively quarrel enlist the sympathies of this or that group in the Galleries; and at the end of the play the whole playhouse becomes an extension of the courtly audience on the Stage watching the lamentable comedy of Pyramus and Thisbe. The critical comments of the Athenian nobility seem to come from the foremost ranks of the audience itself, giving voice to their instinctive reactions; and both the enlightened rebukes of the presiding Duke and the naïve interpolations of Pyramus's running com-

* See *page 46, below.*

mentary are addressed to the whole playhouse as well as to the players on the Stage.

(9) This relationship was emphasised by the fact that the performance took place in the neutral daylight of a London afternoon, the audience and the players being in the same light. Elaborate lighting effects and the deliberate directing of light were impossible: atmosphere, therefore, and subtleties of characterisation and shifting moods were created by other means—the gestures and miming of the actors, and the spoken word, often conveying to the mind's eye what the physical eye could not see. The slow building up through the repetitive imagery of the Moon in the opening scenes of A MIDSUMMER NIGHT'S DREAM to the moment when Oberon cries 'Ill met by Moon-light, proud Titania' is a classic example of the power of Shakespeare's atmospheric creation; and no less remarkable —and equally necessary—is the method by which he dispels the long night through the arrival of the hunting party in Act IV.

(10) The female parts were played by boy-actors, and the illusion of femininity was created by the same means—the words of the dramatist and the intonations, gestures and miming of the players (not only those who played the female parts but also those who acted with them and spoke to and about them). Great subtlety of characterisation was not required of the four boys who had the main female roles in this play. But each of the four is distinguished from the others, and the distinction lies not only in their different circumstances in the narrative but also (and more effectively) in the details of diction, versification, rhythm, lineation, rhyme. We may be sure that the first and most important phase of the boys' apprenticeship was their training in the subtlety of speech. Shakespeare's demands grew ever more exacting, and this fact is in itself evidence of the skill of the boy-players. He would not ask for what he could not expect. It was because Eccleston's shrewish Hermia was so tripping on the tongue that he was given Beatrice before his voice was cracked within the ring; and the promise of these early performances gave Shakespeare the opportunity and the inclination to create Rosalind and Viola and Portia, and the rest.

Now since, in the absence of precise evidence, our reconstruction involves prudent conjecture, we ask the reader to accept as a setting for all that follows the architectural features of the drawing which appears as our frontispiece. A MIDSUMMER NIGHT'S DREAM, as one would expect from its probably extraneous origin, makes little use of the detailed features of the Tiring-House. But it will be helpful to identify the great *Stage* (the main acting arena); the tall broad *Doors* which are the chief means of access to the Stage from the Tiring-House; the discovery-space between the Doors which (for convenience of reference and without any associative intention) we shall call the *Study*; the inset space on the upper level which we shall call the *Chamber*; the two *Stage-Posts* set well forward on the Stage, which will for most of the play's action be accepted as trees in the wood, but for the last Act, hung with candelabra, will become pillars in the great chamber of the Duke's palace; supported by these Posts, the *Heavens* (the painted canopy overhanging the Stage); and the *Trap-Door* in the centre of the Stage, Puck's private bolt-hole and the hearth for the fifth-Act fire; beneath the Trap-Door the *Hell*, from which in this play, instead of the habitual demonic denizens, no one emerges more menacing than Puck with his momentary evocation of sprites let forth from 'the graves, all gaping wide'. Here then, lying between the Heavens and Hell, Shakespeare's Stage is all this world. Above the Heavens are the *Huts*, from which trumpet and banner summon us to the play. All these features we shall bear in mind as we trace the course of the play's action: but while it is easy to over-emphasise the importance of the part played by the minor structural features of the playhouse in the development of Shakespeare's craft, we must never forget that the greater part of the action of each play took place on the bare Stage, and that comparatively little use was made of the other features we have mentioned.

Meanwhile we may isolate three conditions of performance in Shakespeare's theatre which were immutable; and these are of cardinal importance in seeking a full appreciation of his dramatic skills:

(A) a stage or acting area which projected from its background, and on which the action was three-dimensional, like sculpture, not two-dimensional, like painting; so that the audience was closely involved in the action;

(B) a background which was permanent and unchanging, always basically the same (with perhaps different hangings for tragedy, comedy or history, and other adjusted features of furniture or properties to suit the play of the afternoon) and architecturally constant. The audience, entering the playhouse, knew what they would see, and could ignore the features of the background, if the dramatist so wished. The excited interest, at the first performance of each new play, would be—what will they turn it into this time?

(C) a constant and neutral light, embracing players and audience alike, so that illusion of light and darkness, or weather or atmosphere, or subtle characterisation, must be created by the miming, gesture and posture of the actors, and above all by the words which the playwright gave them to speak.

*　　　*　　　*

In such conditions we envisage A MIDSUMMER NIGHT'S DREAM on one of those sundry times when it was publicly acted by the Chamberlain's Men in the daylight of a London afternoon. For our promptbook, we use Fisher's Quarto of 1600, comparing it also with the Folio text of 1623. In quotation, we reproduce, as far as possible without obscuring the sense, the Folio's punctuation and capital letters. The punctuation is the work of several different hands, not least those of the editors, Shakespeare's fellow-players Heminges and Condell; its purpose seems for the most part to be rhetorical rather than syntactical, preserving the fluency and variety of spoken language; it seems to be our nearest approach to the diction of the players, and since it has been filtered through the medium of the player-editors, it may even give us a plainer clue than the Quarto (probably printed from Shakespeare's own manuscript) to the poet's intended phrasing, as it was heard in the playhouse. The Folio's capitals, though they cannot be analysed to represent a system of emphasis, seem nevertheless to reflect from time to time a sense of thematic proportion: it is interesting, for instance, that while they are less frequently deployed than in some other plays, the Folio printer habitually awards a capital to the Moon, the *moonlight = romance & lights the sky & heavens ?*

source of the strongest atmospheric imagery in the play. While we have, for the reader's convenience, made occasional changes, and indeed modernised the spelling throughout, we strongly urge interpreters of Shakespeare, player and student alike, to work from the early printed texts: the quiddities of the Elizabethan and Jacobean printing-houses are no great obstacle to the judicious reader, and under the seemingly eccentric variations of spelling, punctuation, lineation, speech-headings, stage-directions, there lie many clues and trails for the detective who would unravel the mystery of what really happened on the stage of Shakespeare's playhouse.

* * *

Those who adopt the time-honoured view that we know very little about Shakespeare's life, seem to forget that nearly twenty years of it were spent in the whole-time occupation of the playhouse—not only the penning of plays, but rehearsal, training, discussion, adjustment, explanation, improvisation, experiment; and all this among a company of colleagues who were unique in the long endurance and for the most part amicable relationship of their association. Since the range of our speculation covers not only the afternoons of performance but also the mornings of rehearsal, and even the late-night post-mortems at the Mermaid Tavern, it is part of our brief to become acquainted with Shakespeare's fellow-actors, and to let their names grow familiar in the mouth as household words. For this purpose we step still further into the field of conjecture, seeking the aid of Professor Baldwin's book which, besides expounding the facts of the company's organisation, is bold enough to dally with surmise as to the casting of roles. Though we may disagree with this or that ascription, the attempt is valuable, because it keeps us in mind of the fact that the members of the Shakes-pearian company provided among them the first interpreters of these acting roles which are usually discussed as if they existed in abstract independence. Particularly interesting in this play is Baldwin's allot-ment of the parts of Quince and Bottom. For here beside Will Kemp's all-licensed fool, whose practice was to 'set on some quantity of barren Spectators to laugh too, though in the meantime, some necessary Question of the Play be then to be considered', Shakespeare has set an actor of stature and experience in Thomas Pope, a 'sharer' in the company's finances no less than Kemp: so the aspiring tragedian Bottom finds himself curbed by the long-suffering but unyielding author and director Peter Quince. Indeed the whole operation of the mechanicals' unwonted histrionic enterprise is a comic reflection of those morning rehearsals in the playhouse during which the text of Shakespeare's prompt-book came to theatrical life. Interesting too is the subordination in importance (proper to a good repertory company) of the company's 'stars' to their young apprentices—as when in the exuberance of Act III's long quarrel-scene, with Burbage and Condell as their adult foils, the boys Cooke and Eccleston 'carry it away'. Moreover the sharp-pointed caricature of fustian plays in the lamentable comedy of Pyramus and Thisbe is neatly set off by a no less subtle mirror-image of contemporary audiences in which, while Duke Theseus represents the judicious whose opinion is worth a whole theatre of others, his courtiers and indeed his newly-wed bride need to be taught a lesson in enlightened patronage. By keeping in mind the presence and influence of playhouse audience and fellow-players (both in rehearsal and in performance), we have a more vivid impression of the poet himself, ready no doubt to listen to suggestion but, because of his standing as a share-holder in the company, and his unique value as a box-office draw, allowed (is it rash to assume?) to have the last word in decision. It is with such a purpose of evoking the atmosphere of Shakespeare's workshop that we print Baldwin's cast-list for A MIDSUMMER NIGHT'S DREAM: dating the play in the summer of 1594, and therefore some time before the public performance which we postulate, he allots the parts as follows:

Theseus	Phillips
Demetrius	Burbage
Lysander	Condell
Egeus	Heminges
Philostrate	Bryane
Bottom	Kemp
Quince	Pope
Flute	Sly

Hippolyta	Ned Shakespeare
Hermia	Eccleston
Helena	Cooke
Oberon	Goffe
Titania	Gilburne
Puck	Tooley

*   *   *

We need not linger over the exact degree of compromise between classical and Elizabethan styles of dress which the hand-to-mouth method of the Chamberlain's Men's wardrobe could provide to suggest a Greek milieu for Shakespeare's tale. In a familiar passage Granville-Barker (*Prefaces to Shakespeare*, First Series, 128) recommends for a Roman play 'the methods of the Mask and the way of Renaissance painters with classical subjects . . . a mixture, as a rule, of helmet, cuirass, trunk-hose, stockings and sandals, like nothing that ever was worn, but very wearable and delightful to look at'. In the portrayal of civilian life the difference between Renaissance-classical and contemporary costume is almost imperceptible: the ladies, for instance, of the royal family in Veronese's picture of *The Family of Darius before Alexander* (1561) are wearing the attire of the painter's own period. It is by a similar compromise that the Athenian Theseus and his Hippolyta are given by Peter Quince the anachronic titles of 'the Duke and the Duchess' (and in the Fisher Quarto, in the speech-headings of Act V, we have sometimes *Duk.* and *Dutch.*). We may imagine that Hippolyta appeared in Act I and again in Act IV as an Elizabethan great lady, attired for hunting, bow in hand, and booted as befits the Amazon Queen; in Titania's contemptuous phrase she is 'buskin'd'. Against a background of the visual compromise between Elizabethan and classical dress both 'the livery of a Nun' with which Theseus threatens Hermia and 'the Athenian garments' by which Puck must recognise his quarry seem appropriate. And we can accept that elves wear leathern coats, and the Fairy Queen's pensioners gold coats, that cowslips like Elizabethan gallants wear pearl ear-rings, that the mechanicals worry about clean linen and ribbons for their pumps, and have sleeves and hats to be caught by the briars in their panic flight. In this way the costume reflects both the Athenian setting and the countless details in the course of the dialogue which present us with an Elizabethan milieu (a list chosen at random would include the following: the nine men's morris, the scrip and parts of the amateur actors and their tiring-house, the gun's report, the needles working on the sampler, the coats in heraldry, the painted maypole, beef and mustard, churchyards, St. Valentine, sixpence a day, the child playing on his recorder: it will be noticed that the contemporary atmosphere is not confined to the speech of the clowns).

We must pause for longer to consider what the crowded stage at the moment of the first entry of Oberon and Titania looked like in the daylight of a London afternoon. There are rushes on the floor, and leafy boughs upon the Stage-Posts (recently hung there by the first Fairy to appear). The background is still the familiar façade of the Tiring-House, curtained below and above. There are no other visual aids to illusion—except the costumes of the figures (perhaps fifteen of them all told, if we allow six attendants in each train) who throng the Stage. How are they dressed and equipped? We must dismiss from our minds all memories of the conventional fairies of ballet and panto-mime, with their gauzy wings and trim ballet-skirts and tinsel crowns and wands: we must not think of them as female, for the most part: Titania their Queen may have a couple of ladies-in-waiting, but for the rest she is surrounded by a court of Gentlemen—*Mounsieur* Mustardseed (so Bottom addresses him) and *Cavalery* Cobweb—and when she commands them to do her service, she sends them on errands no pretty dancing lady-in-waiting would be asked to undertake: some are to kill cankers in the musk-rose buds; some are to war with rere-mice (that is, bats) for their leathern wings, to make her small elves coats (as dangerous this, you might think, as for mortals to hunt the boar): their offices include keeping back the clamorous owl; one fairy is described as sufficiently venturous to seek the squirrel's hoard and fetch new nuts for Bottom. The opening scene between Oberon and Titania is a downright wrangle, one of those cross-stage slanging-matches with which we are familiar from the early cycle of history plays. It is indeed a civil war, on a miniature scale; and the opposing forces are not children, but miniature grown-ups, their principals

abusively charging each other with adultery and treachery. The immediate cause of the war, the bone of contention, the possession of a
little changeling Indian boy, is trivial enough (as in real life it so often
tragically is), but the effects are disastrous indeed, the upsetting of the
whole course of nature, the progeny of evils which Titania in her
powerful eloquence ascribes to their quarrel, their dissension: 'We are
their parents and original'.

The fairies then are dressed as a miniature copy of the mortals—the
King and Queen a parody of Theseus and Hippolyta, their courtiers
like the gentlemen of Theseus's court; in other words, their style is
fundamentally Elizabethan; and that they should be aware of Elizabethan fashions, in all their rich and extravagant absurdity, seems
plausible enough, since we find them in the last Act of the play lurking
outside the windows of the palace, ready to join Oberon and Titania
in their task of blessing the bridal house. We can think of them as
much intrigued by what they saw on such occasions, and with quick
mimicry, imitating the postures, the gait, the appearance and indeed
the apparel of the courtiers.

And their materials they find in the wood; and moreover in Shakespeare's wood, which is compounded of poetical description and atmospheric colour. Some hints are there for us to find in Shakespeare's text:
the snake's enamelled skin is 'Weed wide enough to wrap a Fairy in':
the leathern wings of bats make coats for Titania's elves: the wings
from painted butterflies serve as fans for Bottom's slumber. Whatever
the property-room may have unearthed for the fairies to wear, it is
clear that Shakespeare conceived of their appearance in the closest
possible relation to their forest home. The accoutrements of Queen
Mab's waggon (ROMEO AND JULIET, I.iv.60 ff.) are imagined by Shakespeare in just the same way: the details of the picture are the empty
hazel-nut, spinners' legs, grasshoppers' wings, cobwebs and a cricket's
bone. Given this kind of hint, we can let our imagination rove.
Peaseblossom admires the soldier's kit: the shape of his leaf gives a
military cut to sleeves and skirt; the helmet comes easily from the
blossom itself; the flat leaf of an iris makes him a well-tempered sword-
blade. It is he that is sent to war with the bats, he that deals firmly
with spotted snakes and thorny hedgehogs, he that stands aloof as

sentinel for the sleeping Queen. Cobweb (shall we say?) has been fascinated by the spectacle of a bishop moving about the palace with downcast eyes and clasped hands. His clerical gown is therefore rigged up from his private store of gossamer, and the petals of a white flower make good Geneva bands. He presides in an attitude of benediction over Titania's lullaby and keeps the beetles at bay with gestures of exorcism. There are many items from the woodland store which fit the wardrobe of an Elizabethan fairy court. Bracken makes a lace collar, an inverted mushroom round the neck makes a capital ruff: the King's sceptre is a sturdy onion-stalk with the seed-pod giving decorative substance of jewellery to the top.

Who is to say that any of these guesses were actual fact in Shakespeare's playhouse? Yet there is evidence to support our conjectures. Poems of fancy about the infinitesimal fairy world became popular in the years after the publication in Quarto of A MIDSUMMER NIGHT'S DREAM. Much ingenuity was spent by the authors in elaborating the costume and equipment of the fairies. No doubt some of the inspiration came from the reading of Shakespeare's text. But it is surely just as likely that the visual appearance of the stage, when the play was being performed, gave rise to some of the details. Typical of these poetical flights is the following passage from William Browne's *Britannia's Pastorals*, quoted by M. W. Latham (*The Elizabethan Fairies*, 209). It is hard to believe that the poet is not describing an actual Oberon in the Jacobean or Caroline theatre:

> Cladd in a sute of speckled gilliflowre.
> His hatt by some choice master in the trade
> Was (like a helmett) of a lilly made.
> His ryffe a daizie was, soe neately trimme,
> As if of purpose it had growne for him.
> His points were of the lady-grasse, in streakes,
> And all were tagg'd, as fitt, with titmouse beakes.
> His girdle, not three tymes as broade as thinne,
> Was of a little trouts selfe-spangled skinne.
> His bootes (for he was booted at that tyde),

Were fittly made of halfe a squirrells hyde,
His cloake was of the velvett flowres, and lynde
With flowre-de-lices of the choicest kinde.

Even where the details are too fanciful to represent stage-properties, at
any rate the tradition of a tiny woodland pastiche of contemporary
court costume seems firmly established. And it persisted: one of the
most elaborate fancies is *King Oberon's Apparel*, a poem by Sir John
Steward, from the 'Musarum Deliciae, or the Muses Recreation',
1656.

This court would not be complete without the King's Jester, who
is Puck; and he will therefore be dressed in a woodland burlesque of
the Fool's motley, and wear on his head the traditional coxcomb—
the head and comb of a farmyard cock flanked with the ears of an ass.
Such a coxcomb can be seen on the title-page of 'A Fooles Bolt is
soone shott' (1614), from Samuel Rowlands's *Complete Works*, 1598–
1628. (The title-page is reproduced in John M. Lothian's *Shakespeare's
Charactery*, facing page 81.) A more traditional picture appears in
Robin Goodfellow, his mad prankes and merry jests, 1628, and may be
found as frontispiece to Latham's book: here Robin is depicted as a
kind of satyr, bearded and horned and with cloven hooves. That
Shakespeare was at least aware of this tradition is suggested by a stage-
direction in the 1602 Quarto of THE MERRY WIVES OF WINDSOR at
V.v.42: *Enter Sir Hugh like a Satyre*: Sir Hugh is later addressed as
Puck by Mistress Quickly. But in A MIDSUMMER NIGHT'S DREAM for the
first time Puck is incorporated into a newly conceived fairy world and
in a particular role: he is Oberon's 'gentle Puck', his confidential
servant, his jester. The model of Tarlton, the famous Fool, is more
appropriate than the satyr's guise. The anonymous author of *Tarltons
Newes out of Purgatorie* ('published by an old companion of his, Robin
Goodfellow') saw in a dream a man 'attired for a clowne', and concluding that it was 'the verye ghoaste of Richard Tarlton . . . fell into
a great feare'. But the ghost smilingly comforted him: 'feare me not,
man, I am but Dick Tarlton, that could quaint it in the court, and
clowne it on the stage. . . . Therefore sith my appearance to thee is in a
resemblance of a spirite, think that I am as pleasant a goblin as the rest,

and will make thee as merry before I part, as ever Robin Goodfellow made the cuntry wenches at their Cream-boules'.

The vein of mock-heroic parody in costume fits the mood of Shakespeare's fairy-story: and we can be the surer that this is the right vein when we remember who were the actors who played the fairy parts. For this play, and for the last Act of THE MERRY WIVES OF WINDSOR, Shakespeare was obliged (we may suppose) to go outside the regular personnel of the Chamberlain's company, and draw upon the children's companies or upon the choristers of a neighbouring choir-school. Choir-boys have a way of looking like cherubs; but for the most part, boys will be boys; and high spirits—their natural prerogative—suppressed under an assumed formality, provide just what is wanted to give life to this section of Shakespeare's cast. While King Oberon and Queen Titania are conducting their vociferous dispute, it is a formal occasion, and their courtiers stand awe-struck in attendance, laughing perhaps when their principal scores a point and countering mockery with hissing and booing; but when the Queen's abrupt departure relaxes the tension, we may imagine them breaking up their groups, exchanging blows or sword-thrusts with the opposition, and scuttling in freakish disorder, like boys just let loose from school. Oberon, Titania and Puck are, of course, trained boy-players of the regular company. Their names (says Baldwin) were Goffe, Gilburne and Tooley. Goffe was Shakespeare's Juliet: what's in a name? A name reminds us that these were real people, that there were talented apprentice-actors for whom Shakespeare thought it worth while to write speeches of much subtlety in content and music. The average height of the assembled fairy court, composed of boy-players and choristers, is appreciably less than the stature of the mortals and reinforces our impression of a world in miniature: but the nature and language of the principals' quarrel is unmistakably adult.

*   *   *

It will not have escaped notice that the unwonted presence of a number of choristers in the playhouse provided Shakespeare with a ready-made choir to supply his musical score. He was not the man to neglect the opportunity, and they were undoubtedly employed (as always for dramatic, not incidental, effect) on at least two occasions in the play. They sing Titania's lullaby, and they sing for the purgation ritual at the end. Whether they were used also as court-musicians to introduce the ducal entry in Act V we do not know: there were madrigals enough available; and they are available still, on the gramophone as well as on the printed page. We do not know what music Shakespeare's company used, but the reader may take a sample by listening to Weelkes's *On the plains, Fairy trains*; the refrain of Pilkington's *Rest, sweet Nymphs* may suggest Titania's lullaby; and the Triumphs of Oriana happily evoke the celebration of Hippolyta's wedding. For the rest, music ('such as charmeth sleep') is called for at a moment of especially lyrical beauty when the King and Queen are newly reconciled and 'rock the ground whereon these sleepers be'. The thrift of an economical book-keeper may, at some performances at least, have turned the boys on to supply this cue as well: let them earn their keep.

*   *   *

But in the end the substance of this play, as of all Shakespeare's plays, is the spoken word of his actors. We need to be constantly reminded that this is almost the whole of his legacy. And because the conditions of his playhouse necessitated a poetic drama, the legacy is all but complete. The text, the full score, of A MIDSUMMER NIGHT'S DREAM is especially rich in poetical devices, as we shall hope to show in the detail of our reconstruction. It is a text for connoisseurs; but such is Shakespeare's artistic tact and sense of theatre that, if the play was indeed originally conceived for an audience of 'the judicious', its wit and charm, when it was transferred to the public playhouse, were not altogether above the heads of the groundlings; moreover in ensuring this success he could rely on the trained skill of his speakers, even (and indeed in this play especially) of his boy-players; as they gave due expression to the comic subtleties of his verbal effects, the shallowest thickskin in the Yard found his ears beguiled and his sense of humour tickled by means which his critical faculty would be at a loss to analyse. There is a constant change of metrical shape and of rhyme-scheme in this text: the courtly mortals usually speak in pentameters, the fairies often (not always) in tetrameters; there are rhyming couplets, and rhyming stanzas of six, sometimes a succession of lines all with the same rhyme; rhyme is used for comic effect, as when Lysander wakes from drugged sleep to supply the second half of Helena's couplet; rhyme is withheld for comic effect in the similar (but differentiated) waking of Demetrius; the long quarrel-scene of the four lovers is conducted mainly in blank verse to achieve a temporary sense of realistic passion; the mechanicals, of course, speak prose, except when in the performance of 'Pyramus and Thisbe' they show Shakespeare's absolute mastery of caricature. Alliteration, assonance, antithesis, balance of phrase against phrase—all the devices of verbal art are employed in this most poetical of Shakespeare's scores. Each choice of style or rhythm is subordinated to the poet's dramatic purpose with an artistic rightness which makes nonsense of Dover Wilson's theory of the survival of a layer of inferior material in Shakespeare's final text.

*   *   *

In one respect A MIDSUMMER NIGHT'S DREAM is unusually interesting: for in the business of the mechanicals' acting company we have illuminating clues to the whole process of Shakespeare's own theatrical activity. Here in a distorting mirror we may see the casting problems of the author accommodating himself to the temperamental awkwardness of his actors, the ambitions of the star, the qualms of the female impersonator, the anxieties of the 'slow of study'; we hear discussion of the need to consider the whims of an audience; we take part in rehearsal; we are finally present at a court performance. Most interesting of all is the pre-rehearsal debate on the methods of creating illusion. Peter Quince's 'two hard things' raise a fundamental issue of the dramatist's art. It is with a characteristically daring stroke of the conjuror's bluff that Shakespeare explicitly states, through the mouth of his 'book-keeper', the problem of how to 'bring the Moon-light into a chamber'. Quince rejects the method of realism, to let the moon shine in through a casement of the chamber-window; he adopts the method of symbolism, and old Starveling, with his bush of thorns and lantern and dog, is cast to 'present the person of Moon-shine'. Meanwhile neither device—neither the realistic nor the symbolical—is the one by which Shakespeare himself has persuaded us to feel, in the afternoon daylight of his playhouse, the presence of the moon. Here is the heart of the mystery, and only by a detailed and continuous reconstruction of the play as performed in the conditions for which Shakespeare made it can we hope to pluck it out.

A MIDSUMMER
NIGHT'S DREAM

[I.i] We cannot easily guess, from the internal evidence of the text, what sort of stage-action was used by the Chamberlain's Men in the opening entry of the play. A suggestion that they represented 'the Return from the Hunt' is no more than a conjecture; but it is dramatically appropriate and, in at least two ways, theatrically convenient—first, that it prepares us for the reappearance of the hunting-party in Act IV, when it is necessary to establish quickly the reason why the Duke and Duchess are out in the wood in the early morning; and secondly, that it helps to deploy the Amazon personality of Hippolyta, whom Titania describes to Oberon as 'the bouncing Amazon, Your buskin'd Mistress, and your Warrior love'; some suggestion of masculinity in her attire is fitting, and this is a reason for her being dressed for hunting; moreover the simile of the 'silver bow, New bent in heaven' may have been reinforced by a gesture pointing to the bow which she has carried and handed to an attendant huntsman; the comparison, besides being appropriate to the personality of Hippolyta, springs with a pleasing fitness from the suggested circumstances of the hunt. For this return from the hunt the Stage, amply strewed with rushes, would seem to represent the space outside the ducal palace. But the effect is mainly created by the costume and equipment of the actors—cloaks, boots, gloves, riding-rods, hunting-spears, bows and quivers, and perhaps the carcase of the quarry, a deer carried in triumph on a pole. Such a scene would be parallel to that presented in AS YOU LIKE IT, IV.ii, where the quizzical Jaques says bitterly of the successful Lord who killed the deer: 'Let's present him to the Duke like a Roman conqueror'. In whatever way the scene was visually presented, we may be sure that the Chamberlain's Men were quick to follow the points of emphasis, the guide-lines of our expectation, prescribed so surely by the playwright in his opening speeches.

[1-19]   The first words, **Now fair Hippolyta, our nuptial hour Draws on apace,** evoke for the educated section of the audience a familiar context of Greek legend. *The Knight's Tale* of Chaucer starts with a paragraph describing how Theseus 'weddede the queene Ypolita, And broughte hire hoom with hym in his contree With muchel glorie and greet solempnytee'. The cognoscenti therefore in the Galleries are quickly immersed in the circumstances of the story: and the penny stinkards in the Yard are not at a loss for long. For though the principal actors this afternoon are wearing that compromise between the classical and the Elizabethan styles of clothing which is exemplified in illustrations of the period and in the paintings of Veronese and Titian and Tintoretto, they know by the dialogue that we are in ancient Greece, and they are used to the fact that Shakespeare's imagination, like that of the painters, habitually conceived of his story in terms of contemporary life: we are reminded of this double vision by the fact that Theseus, almost at once, is addressed as 'our renowned Duke'.

The points of emphasis are quickly and clearly defined—the forthcoming wedding (**our nuptial hour**); and the tedious interval in between, lingering the lovers' desires, an interval which is to be relieved by **the pert and nimble spirit of mirth**; and (unmistakably stressed) **the Moon**. It is fruitless to begin calculating (from the armchair) that in the sequel there are not **four happy days** before the wedding, and that, if the old moon is waning and the new moon still four days off, there is no moon to speak of in the interval. This nicety of calculation misconceives the method of Shakespeare's poetic drama. The moon is a principal element in his pervasive imagery—that blend of poetical suggestion and association and overtone which creates the atmospheric harmony of the play. The Athenian court, the city craftsmen, the fairies—all speak frequently, and sometimes elaborately, about the moon. The presence of the moon is felt throughout the first three Acts of the play, and it seems likely that right from the start the Chamberlain's Men established in the mind's eye of the audience a particular direction, a particular angle of the playhouse roof where the moon would seem to be shining: and it would be from an opposite angle that, towards the end of the third Act, we should be made to imagine the coming of daylight, the shining of 'Aurora's harbinger' (III.ii.380). Certainly in his first few lines Theseus seems to point, with a gesture or an inclination of the head, as he sighs his impatience:

> **but oh, methinks, how slow**
> **This old Moon wanes . . .**

Such a method of evocation of what cannot be seen is a necessary feature of the actors' skill in the neutral daylight of the Elizabethan playhouse. The necessity bred many of Shakespeare's most eloquent inventions. Meanwhile, there is a faint sense of collusion in these opening speeches, as if the actors, like a conventional prologue, promise the audience an interval of mirth, an assurance that they will quickly **dream** away the time.

[20-127]   Philostrate, recognisably the major-domo, the Master of the Revels, has gone by one of the Stage-Doors upon his errand, to 'stir up the Athenian youth to merriments': the entry of Egeus is made from the other Door. In Chaucer, Theseus's approach to Athens, 'with victorie and with melodye', is interrupted by a kneeling deputation of mourning widows. Likewise in Shakespeare's play, the 'nimble spirit of mirth' finds its counterpoint of **vexation** and **complaint**. The overtones of reminiscence, especially in the first moments of a play before the mood is firmly established, contribute to the receptive re-action of the educated audience. (We have to remember that this play, perhaps because it was originally devised for a courtly audience on a festival occasion, is subtle and allusive:[1] its appeal is more to the connoisseur than to the groundlings; they are, it is true, well catered for in the scenes of the mechanicals, but there too the essence of the joke is a high-brow one: it hardly needs saying that the absurdity of the performance of 'Pyramus and Thisbe' depends not only upon farcical clowning but also upon the wit of verbal caricature. In this respect, as in others, the play is of a kind with LOVE'S LABOUR'S LOST.) Instead, however, of the lamenting suppliants of Chaucer, Shakespeare's intruder is the familiar figure of the indignant father—familiar for its

similar manifestation in the character of old Capulet, familiar also in the person of John Heminges, whose skill in representing outraged parenthood owed something perhaps to his own home-life (with a family of more than a dozen children), and certainly helped Shakespeare in the creation of a whole line of kindred figures, including Glendower, Polonius and Brabantio. Even in the comparatively brief role of Hermia's father, it is possible to observe how the voice and personality and mannerisms of Heminges kindled his poet-colleague's imagination to express character in living speech. There is a vigour and verisimilitude in his tirade which brings the scene to immediate life. The prompt naming of the new-comers is of course a simple form of exposition for the convenience of the audience, but it is also phrased with the individual tones that build character and situation: **my child, my daughter Hermia** hints at a habit of repetition which comes to full comic exaggeration in the eternally re-phrased definitions of Polonius: self-righteous anger is aptly expressed in the formal balance of

> **Stand forth Demetrius. My noble Lord,**
> **This man . . .**

and

> **Stand forth Lysander. And my gracious Duke,**
> **This man . . .**[2]

The aggressive hammering of **Thou, thou Lysander, thou . . .**, the scornful mockery of the line **With feigning voice, verses of feigning love** (the alliterative 'v' reinforcing the repeated 'f'), the lively caricature of that catalogue of **messengers Of strong prevailment in unhard'ned youth,** the return from direct assault upon the young offender to a renewed obsequious appeal to **my gracious Duke**, the heightening seriousness as the father invokes against his daughter **the ancient privilege of Athens**—all these details of verbal bravura build to a climax of sudden shock:

> **. . . either to this Gentleman,**
> **Or to her death . . .**

and a moment of silent astonishment on stage and in the playhouse follows Egeus's cadence. Playwright and actor have their will: the interest of the audience is aroused; they want to know more about this group of four, who are appealing for the judgement of the Duke. The kneeling figure of the daughter—a boy-player, short of stature, dressed as an Elizabethan lady in puffed sleeves and a farthingale— evokes more than interest: all but the disenchanted hearts of crabbed age will feel sympathy for her predicament.

Theseus, as his legendary character would lead us to expect, is temperate in his judgement, and gracious in expressing it: but its substance is uncompromising:

> **What say you, Hermia? be advis'd, fair Maid,** *aspect of*
> **To you your Father should be as a God . . .** *parental love*

and the actor's eloquent hands illustrate the modelling image of his comparison:

> **. . . you are but as a form in wax**
> **By him imprinted: and within his power,**
> **To leave the figure, or disfigure it.**

Hermia's response is at first nicely balanced between respectful **modesty In such a presence** and the unknown **power**—the pressure of her love—which makes her **bold** to know

> **The worst that may befall me in this case,**
> **If I refuse to wed Demetrius.**

The Duke's prompt answer, **Either to die the death . . .**, repeats the phrasing of her father's merciless demand; and the shock of that ominous word is reflected in the dismay of Lysander's reaction. But then, with the wisdom of Solomon, Theseus provides an alternative, more appropriate to the circumstances: **to abjure For ever the society of men** by taking the vows of the convent. And using the method of the

no love 'fruitless'

poetic drama, Shakespeare gives substance to that alternative by painting it vividly in words:

For aye to be in shady Cloister mew'd,
To live a barren sister all your life,
Chanting faint hymns to the cold fruitless Moon.

A glance at the established quarter of the playhouse roof reminds us of the prevailing presence of the moon, which is here enriched with the classical associations of virginity and chastity. This element of the play's pervasive imagery grows gradually, hint by hint, in the unconscious imagination of the audience. Still graciously and tactfully advising, the Duke warns the young head-strong girl, with another metaphor, from the growth of the rose, how hard it is to **undergo such maiden pilgrimage**: and when she continues defiant, he checks her heroic resolve by offering her a respite, **Take time to pause**, until **the next new Moon**: on that day she must make her choice: the three possibilities remain—to die, to marry Demetrius, or to make her vow of celibacy **on Diana's Altar**. 'The next new Moon' is to be the Duke's own wedding-day: he has already bidden his Master of the Revels to 'Turn melancholy forth to Funerals: The pale companion is not for our pomp'. It is a strange day for Hermia's life-and-death decision.

We now hear the two suitors for the first time. If we accept Baldwin's conjectures, Demetrius speaks with the voice of Burbage; Lysander is Henry Condell, from early days an active and versatile member of the company, and to be Heminges's collaborator in editing the Folio of 1623. This is a play of no star-parts, but we are reminded by the presence of Burbage of the solidarity of this industrious repertory company, required to provide a different play on each of six afternoons in the week. Lysander's wit does something to qualify the note of doom:

You have her father's love, Demetrius:
Let me have Hermia's: do you marry him.

And when he goes on to reveal that Demetrius has been paying court

to another lady, we are ready to laugh outright at the discomfiture of
this spotted and inconstant man. Lysander's description of Helena's
infatuation is exorbitantly alliterative: **. . . she (sweet Lady) dotes,
Devoutly dotes, dotes in Idolatry. . . .** And it prepares us for some
absurdity of excess in that lady's passion, when we meet her. The
Duke's final speech in this opening scene also helps to palliate the
grimness of the mood: for though he repeats his judgement with
emphasis, the transition to a lighter vein is too abrupt to be uninten-
tional:

> **. . . the Law of Athens yields you up**
> **(Which by no means we may extenuate)**
> **To death, or to a vow of single life.**
> **Come my Hippolyta, what cheer my love?**

Hermia's dilemma need not disturb his newly-arrived bride-to-be: he
offers a reassurance of his intention to turn melancholy forth to funerals.

[128-179]   After the Duke's departure, the mood changes from a
public occasion to a private conversation, and the style changes likewise to suit the mood. The variations of style in this play are for the
most part skilfully calculated and an important element in the dramatic
coherence of the whole composition. They have, quite rightly, been
treated as evidence of revision: but in analysing this evidence, critics
have made a fairly general assumption that the greater the formality
of the diction and versification, the earlier the date of composition, and
(as a corollary) the worse the work of the playwright.[3] We are con-
sidering the text of the Fisher Quarto, which we take to be Shakespeare's final version after revision: and we are guessing that he was
satisfied with the final form of his text, that the supposedly 'primitive'
and 'inferior' passages were left by him deliberately side by side with
the new material, and that any contrast in style was calculated, to suit
the shifting moods and different content of the play's episodes. The
lyrical vein of the first half of the present conversation between the
lovers is a deliberate artifice: it does not deny the spontaneous feeling
of the speakers; it enriches it and gives it a universal appeal. Hermia,
after the Duke's judgement, is left pale with anger and frustration: she

is not weeping, but is on the brink of tears. This is expressed by balanced (though unrhymed) couplets in the shapely terms of poetical conceit:

> How now my love? Why is your cheek so pale?
> How chance the Roses there do fade so fast?
> —Belike for want of rain, which I could well
> Beteem them, from the tempest of my eyes.

It is Shakespeare's intention (in avoiding the depths of personal tragedy) that Lysander should relate their experience to the general context of **tale or history**, observing in a memorable line that

> **The course of true love never did run smooth.**

Then follows a formal antiphon, rhythmically marked by Hermia's impulsive interjections—**O cross! . . . O spite!. . . O hell!**—itemising three age-old problems of incompatible love. Lysander caps this exchange by dilating on the tragic accidents which foil even mutual love, the love that springs from **a sympathy in choice**:[4] the strands of his imagery (the **shadow**, the **dream**, the **lightning in the collied night**) help to weave the texture of the ensuing story; and his summing-up, still within the lyrical frame, draws a picture of sadness common to all mortals:

> **So quick bright things come to confusion.**

Hermia accepts their frustration as **an edict in destiny**, and her patient resignation wins our sympathy while at the same time suggesting a native and habitual absurdity in the recurring predicament of lovers: theirs is

> **a customary cross,**
> **As due to love, as thoughts, and dreams, and sighs,**
> **Wishes and tears; poor Fancy's followers.**

It is a charming dialogue, and after the potentially tempestuous issues of tragedy raised by the plaintiff father and the ducal judge, these thirty lines have steered us safely into the calmer waters of comedy.

In formal verse of haunting sweetness Hermia and Lysander have touched on the immemorial problems of lovers without the particularity of self-indulgence. Now mood and style change with Lysander's brisk exposition of his plan of elopement. Factual information is positively expressed—a **Widow Aunt . . . Of great revenue . . . no child . . . seven leagues** from Athens, beyond the reach of **the sharp Athenian Law**. Only when we are asked to contemplate the coming *mise-en-scène* does the poet charge his brush with atmospheric colour: **tomorrow night . . . in the wood . . . (Where I did meet thee once with Helena, To do observance to a morn of May) There will I stay for thee**. It is merely the beginning of a process, developed subsequently with more and more elaboration, which will turn the bare Stage of the playhouse into a moonlit wood. Hermia's reply, with its mounting invocation of the stock declarations of lovers, culminates in a couplet of explicit mockery, the last word of its first line delayed to give calculated surprise:

> **By all the vows that ever men have broke**
> **(In number more than ever women spoke) . . .**

By the end of the speech, we shall have become aware that her couplets rhyme. On the printed page, we can observe that she slips into rhyming only with her fourth and fifth lines. The gear-change is planned to be smooth and imperceptible. These are the first rhymes of the play. In the sequel there is much subtle use of rhyme-schemes and metrical devices. The effect here is to accentuate the gathering irony of Hermia's catalogue of lovers' vows. It also prepares us for the teasing comedy of Helena's first appearance.

[179-225] Lysander, in an unrhymed line, draws attention to the new arrival—a taller, gawkier boy-player, sprinting with long-legged strides from one Door to the other. Helena is running in pursuit of her fickle lover. Hermia's voice checks her flight, and Helena's prompt retort establishes at once the bantering tone of the sequel. Pouncing on her friend's perfunctory epithet, **fair Helena**, she toys with the word, like a kitten with a ball; she caps Hermia's line with a rhyme; and thereafter the rest of the scene is written in rhyming pairs of lines, sometimes with the sense overrunning the couplet, sometimes with the epigrammatic force of the couplet's cadence. Especially delightful, and irresistibly comic, are the ten lines of stichomythia, in which Helena's rueful comments match the other's amused self-justification. Sometimes she echoes herself:

> **O that your frowns . . .**
> **O that my prayers . . .**

Sometimes she manipulates Hermia's formula:

> **The more I hate, the more he follows me.**
> **—The more I love, the more he hateth me.**

The boy-player quickly establishes a figure of likeable absurdity. The quick-fire interchange ends with comfort from Hermia: she and Lysander tell Helena of their plan to elope. Their informative speeches fall into groups of six lines (three couplets from Hermia; three from Lysander, unexpectedly betraying his hitherto unseen presence from Helena's other side; then three more from Hermia). The formality of the poet's pattern makes it inevitable that Hermia should take up the tale after Lysander's six lines:

> **Through Athens gates, have we devis'd to steal . . .**
> **—And in the wood, where often you and I . . .**

and Helena's head, bobbing from left to right, and back again, marks the regular transition from speaker to speaker. We may be sure that the Chamberlain's Men, boy-players as well as adults, were taught to observe and reproduce the pattern of the poet's dialogue. The movement is rounded off with a farewell group of six lines, but divided this time between the two speakers.

Meanwhile the pervasive atmosphere of the wood and moonlight is further developed in prospect: a vivid pictorial image strikes the mind's eye of the listener:

> **Tomorrow night, when Phoebe doth behold**
> **Her silver visage, in the wat'ry glass,**
> **Decking with liquid pearl the bladed grass . . .**

and the speaker's glance helps to reinforce the effect by taking in that angle of the playhouse roof which we are already beginning to associate with the presence of the moon. The **faint Primrose beds**, where in times past the two girls **were wont to lie**, add a detail to the picture, and **morrow deep midnight** rouses still further our expectation of darkness on the daylit Stage.

[226-251]   When we envisage the first Helena holding his audience in the public playhouse with his soliloquy, we must remember the probably early date of the first version of this play and calculate the poet's expectation of his boy-players at this stage of his writing career. The passionate tirades of Queen Margaret and Tamora, the subtle defensive word-play of Richard Crookback's female victims, the cut-and-thrust of the Shrew's resistance to her tamer, the sets of wit well played by the Princess of France and her mocking wenches, the gentle pathos of Julia and the tragic eloquence of Juliet—all these diverse kinds of women's speech were for the most part framed in regular verse-patterns and pointed with the orthodox tricks of rhetoric. The training of the apprentice-actors, rigorous as the exercises in theory and practice of the professional musician, was designed to perfect the eloquence of their voices. And so successful was this training in individual cases—we know the names of some of these young virtuosi, Goffe, Eccleston, Gilburne, Ned Shakespeare, Crosse, Edmans—that the poet gradually raised his demands, and created for these voices the subtle seeming-spontaneous prose of Beatrice and Rosalind, the heart-rending incoherence of mad Ophelia and sleepless Lady Macbeth, the infinite variety of Cleopatra's unprecedented flexible and all-expressive music. But as yet, when he wrote for Helena and Hermia, he expected no more than a virtuosity of pointed verse-speaking and the ability to express situation and mood and character by verbal dexterity. So

now Helena, alone for the moment on the Stage among an audience of mixed tastes and expectations, holds forth in elegantly turned rhyming couplets on the notorious blindness of love. As with Hermia and Lysander, her particular predicament is placed in context of the old tales and conventions. There is little original in what she says, but much to admire in the way she, and the poet, say it. The argument is conducted with a kind of naïve logic:

> **Love looks not with the eyes, but with the mind,**
> **And therefore is wing'd Cupid painted blind.**
> **Nor hath love's mind of any judgement taste:**
> **Wings and no eyes figure unheedy haste.**
> **And therefore is Love said to be a child,**
> **Because in choice he is so oft beguil'd . . .**

love
is
blind

and the naïvety is a reflection of the speaker's personality. We cannot help smiling at her simple acceptance of the error of her infatuation, and the image by which she describes the fickleness of Demetrius is unmistakably comic in the petulantly plaintive tone of her denouement:

> **For ere Demetrius look'd on Hermia's eyne,**
> **He hail'd down oaths that he was only mine.**
> **And when this Hail some heat from Hermia felt,**
> **So he dissolv'd, and showers of oaths did melt.**

When she turns to plain exposition of her intention to tell her beloved of **fair Hermia's flight** and the ingenuous motive of her betrayal, Shakespeare breaks the epigrammatic couplet-structure by overrunning the line:

> **Then to the wood will he, tomorrow night,**
> **Pursue her . . .**

but for the cadence of Helena's little aria he returns to the formality of a final couplet. The boy-player will know from his training the

theatrical value of this familiar device: the bare Stage of the Elizabethan playhouse has neither the descending curtain nor the expedient
blackout which may in the modern theatre mark the conclusion of an
episode; one of the many uses of rhyme is to ring, as it were, a final
bell in the dialogue before the player makes his way to the Door by
which he leaves the Stage.

*   *   *

[I.ii] Hitherto the appeal of the play has been mostly to the judicious;
it has been caviare to the general, and the interest of the groundlings,
and indeed of the injudicious undoubtedly to be found in the Galleries,
has been somewhat underfed. So a wave of contented anticipation will
ripple the surface of the Yard, when the Chamber-curtains open to
reveal the familiar members of the company's comedy gang dressed,
like many of the groundlings themselves, in the leather jerkins and
aprons of Elizabethan craftsmen. Prominent among them is the unmistakable figure of Will Kemp, star comedian of the Chamberlain's
Men, whose mere appearance on stage is sure to set the playhouse on
a roar. Some of his colleagues too have become well enough known to
the playhouse audience as his regular supporting stooges and 'feeds'.
But one of his fellows this afternoon is an actor of tried accomplish-
ment and versatility, Thomas Pope, whose character of **Peter Quince**
is first to be named in the course of the dialogue. The decision to set
up Pope in opposition to Kemp is significant. He played Buckingham
to Burbage's Richard Crookback and Mercutio to his Romeo, and
showed a flair for the comic-fantastic as Armado: and his histrionic
range is attested by his subsequent 'creation' of so wide a variety of
roles as Shylock, Falstaff, Fluellen and Jaques. This list of Pope's parts
is again from the conjectural cast-lists of Baldwin. Shakespeare, thus
early, shows that disapproval of unlicensed fooling which finds its explicit expression in Hamlet's rebuke to self-indulgent clowns. By a
stroke of diplomatic genius, he makes the ebullient Kemp caricature
himself as the egocentric Bottom and places beside him Pope, an actor
of his own calibre, as Peter Quince who, however primitive he may be
as author and book-keeper, has a proper regard for the artistic
disciplines of the players' company.

That the scene was placed in the Chamber is, of course, conjecture. It could equally well have taken place on the lower level; indeed in private performance an upper level may well not have been available. But there is no reason to suppose that private and public performances were exactly alike in the details of presentation, and it is with performance in the public playhouse that we are concerned. The mechanicals represent a strand of the play strikingly different from the others, and it is appropriate that they should have at first their own recognisable home away from the main traffic of the Stage. The audacity of their excursions, first into the wood where they become entangled with the fairy world, and then into the ducal palace where they mix with the gentry of the play, is heightened in performance by their departure from their base. The use of the Chamber allows us to feel in two little scenes (I.ii and IV.ii) that the mechanicals are distinctively at home; and it is significant that these two scenes flank the long sequence in the wood which contains the chief action of the play. As in other plays, the visual contrast is helpful in supporting the contrast in the poet's dramatic structure and style: the movement from the confines of the Chamber to the open Stage reflects the change from homely Athens to the fantastic world of the wood.

[I-115] *Enter Quince, the Carpenter; and Snugge, the Joyner; and Bottom, the Weaver; and Flute, the Bellowes mender; & Snout, the Tinker; and Starveling the Tayler.* The minute detail of the Quarto's direction is reproduced in the Folio, and it is clear that some emphasis is laid upon the various trades of the craftsmen: their daily occupations are marked, we may suppose, by visible properties: Bottom, for instance, fingers with professional interest the cloth upon which Starveling is plying his needle and thread; Flute uses a pair of bellows, which he is mending, to blow down the neck of Snug, whose strident saw is drowning Quince's attempts to draw the attention of **all our company**. The furnishings of the Chamber—carpenter's bench, joint-stools, planks and mallet—locate us firmly in Quince's shop. Shakespeare's intention is to present for us the humdrum routine of his 'rude Mechanicals' and then to create drama by superimposing upon this routine the incongruity of their immediate preoccupation with the arts. He wastes no time in informing us: in a dozen lines we know that these craftsmen

are planning an **Interlude before the Duke and the Duchess, on
his wedding day at night** (we have already heard, of course, that
this will be on 'the next new Moon'), and we are told the subject of
the interlude, **the most lamentable Comedy, and most cruel
death of Pyramus and Thisbe.** It is a situation ripe for laughter, for
the entertainment of Galleries and groundlings alike: it is as if the
groundlings themselves were putting together a play for performance
at court: and if the joke is going to be largely at the groundlings'
expense, that is no hardship; for always it is your neighbour rather than
yourself who is the fool. The joke is that on stage the craftsmen themselves do not see the joke: they take their task of entertaining the Duke
and Duchess seriously. A critic says of them later in the play that they
'never labour'd in their minds till now'. The intellectual effort is hard
for them: their wrinkled brows and bewildered looks, their alterna-
tions of optimism and despair, their admiration of Bottom's virtuosity,
and his own inventive assurance, all show them to be in deadly earnest.
Not even Kemp succumbs to the 'most pitiful Ambition' of playing
for laughs: for Bottom takes himself seriously as an actor; and Kemp
must earn for him the uncritical confidence of his fellow-players, and
Quince's subsequent opinion of him: 'You have not a man in all
Athens, able to discharge Pyramus but he.'

Shakespeare has taken special pains with this sextet of comedians, as
indeed he has done before with a set of a different genre, the village
characters of LOVE'S LABOUR'S LOST, who also undertake to entertain
the court with a theatrical show. The success of the earlier play no
doubt prompted the repetition on a more ambitious scale of the burlesque dénouement. A principal cause for both successes is the fact that
we are encouraged to know the amateur players in their own characters
first, before we see them in their assumed roles. Pompey the Great is
funny because we know Costard, his impersonator: we have enjoyed
the company of the mild curate, Sir Nathaniel, and would expect him
to prove 'a little o'er-parted' in the role of Alexander: and when as
Judas Maccabaeus he is put out of countenance by the mocking courtiers, the dignified rebuke of Holofernes, 'This is not generous, not
gentle, not humble', is wholly right in character for the village peda-
gogue who has for many years ruled over the children of his social

47

superiors at the charge-house on top of the mountain, 'or *Mons* the hill'. In this play too the burlesque absurdities of 'Pyramus and Thisbe' would be far less funny if we did not relate each character in the 'lamentable Comedy' to the previously sketched personality of its impersonator. We are introduced to each of Quince's five colleagues, with mention of both name and trade, by the simple device of having him **call them generally, man by man, according to the scrip.**

Nick Bottom the Weaver is of course first **by the scroll**, unquestionably the leading member of the company; and no one is surprised that the **part** he is **for** is the title-role, that he is **set down for Pyramus.** To Bottom's mind the hero must be one of two things— **a lover, or a tyrant.** Quince, knowing Bottom of old and foreseeing his predilection for the latter type, the more robust and ostentatious tyrant, is at pains to allure him with a note of reassurance: Pyramus is something more than a lover, he has tragic stature; **a lover that kills himself, most gallant, for love.** The commas, eloquent of tendentious blarney, come from the Fisher Quarto. Bottom is at first rapt in contemplation of the great performance he will give as the tragic lover; and he carries his companions with him as they imagine how the audience must **look to their eyes**, while Pyramus will **move storms** and **condole in some measure.** Then he bids Quince proceed **to the rest.** But before Quince can frame the name of Francis Flute on his lips, Bottom breaks out again to voice his regret for an opportunity lost: **my chief humour is for a tyrant. I could play Ercles rarely....** His impromptu performance of a passage inaccurately remembered but brilliantly improvised to supply both metre and rhyme—

> **And Phibbus' car**
> **Shall shine from far,**
> **And make and mar**
> **The foolish Fates**

—will strike even the unlettered as funny, and flatter them with the knowledge that they can distinguish ham-acting from the real thing. But Bottom's fellow-craftsmen do not share the joke at his expense: to them there is no question but that **This was lofty.** To the cognoscenti

the joke was subtler; for they would know that the extravagant style of
Bottom's outburst is a by no means distant parody of passages which
had been heard (and could still be heard) in the public theatres of the
time.[5] But Shakespeare's comedy, even when its ultimate appeal is to
an esoteric audience, never (not even among the driest enigmas of
LOVE's LABOUR's LOST) strays far from the apprehension of the groundlings, who can be aware of the existence of a comic situation, even
when they cannot understand the words in which it is developed.
Now name the rest of the Players, says Bottom, well satisfied with
the impression he has made upon his admiring friends: and again
Quince begins to articulate the name of Francis Flute. But Bottom
again interrupts with a post-script; it must not be thought, because he
is good at tyrants, that he cannot tackle the lover, and he repeats with
complacency the *mot juste* which previously suggested itself to his artistic taste: **a lover is more condoling.** The long-drawn 'o' of the
epithet, matched with a suitably lugubrious countenance, is as absurd
to us in the audience as it is impressive to his colleagues.

At last, and after an eloquently sarcastic pause, in case Bottom should
feel disposed to start up yet again, the patient chairman proceeds to the
next name on the agenda, **Francis Flute the Bellows-mender.** Flute
is, of course, the youngest among the craftsmen: he has **a beard
coming**—but it has not come yet. Throwing himself momentarily
into what he thinks is the posture of knight-errantry, he is crest-fallen
to hear that Thisbe is not **a wand'ring Knight** but **the Lady that
Pyramus must love.** The laughter of his fellows accentuates his discomfiture, and the ray of hope when Bottom offers to **play Thisbe
too** is soon extinguished by the sharp tongue of the director. Bottom's
enthusiasm spreads its infection in the Yard, the absurdity of his
demonstration of how to **speak in a monstrous little voice** is certain to bring the house down, and his satisfaction at having made a
hit with his audience is only partially damped by the severity of
Quince's call to order. The scene is an echo of what must have happened
often enough at the morning's rehearsal in the playhouse, when Kemp's
unrepentant exuberance taxed the patience of the book-keeper. For
Quince's function in the play is that of the book-keeper—holding the
prompt-book, distributing the parts, collecting the properties, con-

ducting the rehearsals. As Quince knows how to handle Bottom, with a mixture of cajolery and firmness, so the book-keeper of the Chamberlain's Men will have learnt the best way to manipulate the temperamental genius of Kemp: and Pope's past observation of rehearsals makes him a vivid interpreter of the book-keeper's diplomatic role.[6]

Robin Starveling the Tailor looks like a part for Dick Cowley. Though Baldwin, putting a very early date to A MIDSUMMER NIGHT'S DREAM, does not assign the part to Cowley, he is known to have been Verges to Kemp's Dogberry, and other roles assigned to him in Baldwin's lists are Robert Faulconbridge (in KING JOHN) whose legs are 'two such riding rods' and whose arms are 'eel-skins stuff'd', Old Gobbo, Silence, William (in AS YOU LIKE IT), Aguecheek and Slender: Cowley, Baldwin tells us, 'seems to have been decidedly thin, and to have capitalized this characteristic for comic effect'. Advanced age and a touch of deafness make it difficult for Starveling to take in his assignment of **Thisbe's mother**. In the event, his destiny is far more glorious. **Tom Snout, the Tinker** likewise has a more rewarding opportunity than **Pyramus' father**. Apparently **Snug the Joiner** (alone of the six, he is never vouchsafed his first name) is the dimmest-witted of the party: by his own ingenuous confession, he is **slow of study**, slower still in his desire to have **the Lion's part written**: he too however is to earn his meed of praise for the single-minded integrity of his performance. The laughter at his expense, when Quince drily reassures him (**You may do it extempore, for it is nothing but roaring**), is drowned by the interruption of the irrepressible Bottom, who wants to **play the Lion too**. Kemp's comic skill has yet another manifestation as he imitates (not once only, but a second time, to improve on the first) the aristocratic accents of the Duke: **Let him roar again, let him roar again.** Quince, patient still, counters Bottom's suggestion with the ingenious argument, put forward in all seriousness, that Bottom's performance would be so realistic as to **fright the Duchess and the Ladies**, and the whole company are genuinely concerned lest **That would hang us, every mother's son.** Perhaps the audience would see a topical allusion here to an actual incident, when a lion was removed from a triumphal procession at the Scottish court 'because his presence might have brought some feare to the nearest' (the incident is described in the *New Cambridge* edition, 95). However that may be (and it is typical of Shakespeare's invention to draw upon topical events to keep the pot of comedy on the boil), Bottom has a remedy—and we begin to realise that this is characteristic of the bland optimism and assurance with which Shakespeare has invested his personality. Again Kemp's chameleon voice will show us how to **roar you as gently as any sucking Dove**. And at last Quince loses patience: his hammer on the carpenter's bench adds finality to the book-keeper's ruling: **You can play no part but Pyramus**. There is a pause of crisis, while Bottom sulks, and the consternation of his colleagues affects even Quince. He turns to wheedling, and the epithets with which he baits his hook of persuasion rise in a series to a climax: **a sweet-fac'd man, a proper man . . . a most lovely Gentleman-like man: therefore you** (the pronoun is emphatic) **must needs play Pyramus**. The suspense, almost unbearable, lest Bottom will not play, is broken, with sighs of relief, by his lofty, condescending acceptance: **Well, I will undertake it**. There is a touch of sly comedy in the immediate sequel, of Bottom's naïve concern for the **beard** it were **best to play it in**, and the almost contemptuous unconcern of Quince, once he has gained his point: **Why, what you will**. As he winds up the meeting, the book-keeper distributes the parts, having appointed a time and place for rehearsal, and sits down to **draw a bill of properties, such as our play wants**. In fixing the venue, he adds a touch or two of atmospheric colour such as Shakespeare's play wants: **. . . tomorrow night . . . in the palace wood, a mile without the Town, by Moon-light . . . At the Duke's oak we meet**. Quince has conducted his casting-session with an admirably insistent relevance: the quality belongs to Shakespeare himself, Quince's creator. There is no need, and no room, for irrelevant business or impromptu clowning in the scene. Shakespeare has shown exemplary tact, for the irrelevant clowning of Bottom is a necessary question of the play: and its control by Quince is equally relevant. By giving the part of Bottom to Kemp he has insured the exuberance, and by opposing Pope in the part of Quince he has given due weight to the restraining voice of the chairman.

*   *   *

And so it seems that first Hermia and Lysander, and then Helena after Demetrius, and finally the company of mechanicals will all, for their various reasons, make their way to the moonlit wood. When we know, as we soon shall do, that they will find other company there before them, we shall feel that the materials of a comedy have been assembled. The strands, thus presented separately, will be delicately woven together.

*　　*　　*

[II.i] Shakespeare then turns to the third and last part of his exposition, and the seeming ease with which he achieves his purpose should not blind us to the formidable difficulty of the task he set himself—to create on the rush-strewn Stage against the familiar background of the Tiring-House in afternoon daylight the illusion of the moonlit fairy-haunted wood in which the greater part of the action of the play takes place. It seems likely (for reasons that will appear later) that the curtains of the Study-space remain closed for the first episodes of the woodland sequence: the poet's powers are accordingly the more severely taxed. There were other fairy-plays before Shakespeare's,[7] but this is the first time (apart from incidental phenomena like La Pucelle's Fiends and Margery Jourdain's conjured Spirit) that he has brought supernatural characters on to his Stage. It is well known that there are links between consecutive plays suggesting that, during the writing of one play, Shakespeare's mind was already reaching towards the next: JULIUS CAESAR and HAMLET have such an association; so too MACBETH and ANTONY AND CLEOPATRA. We cannot be certain whether ROMEO AND JULIET or A MIDSUMMER NIGHT'S DREAM is the earlier play; but the story of ROMEO AND JULIET seems to be reflected in parody in the 'most lamentable Comedy . . . of Pyramus and Thisbe', and in one passage Shakespeare lets his imagination wander over the detail of the fairy world: Mercutio's cadenza on the equipage and the activities (as mischievous as Puck's) of Queen Mab (ROMEO AND JULIET, I.iv. 55 ff.) provides an informative clue to Shakespeare's treatment of the fairy theme—knitting both fantasy and earth-bound reality—in A MIDSUMMER NIGHT'S DREAM:[8] it is not insignificant that, when Mercutio is interrupted by Romeo's 'Thou talk'st of nothing', he retorts: 'True, I talk of dreams: Which are the children of an idle brain,

Begot of nothing, but vain fantasy'. In his fuller exploration of the world of fairies, Shakespeare deliberately roused the expectation of his audience by summoning them to witness a Dream, and he invoked further overtones in their minds by relating his dream-play to Midsummer Night—'midsummer madness' and the mysterious influence of spirits upon those who wander at that season in the woods at night.

[1-59]   What then happens when the Chamber-curtains have closed upon Quince's carpenter's shop? The first Fairy to appear, *at one doore*, is probably (but not certainly) female, a lady-in-waiting on the Fairy Queen. She (a boy-player with a trained voice, perhaps having his first chance to exercise it in public) comes from one of the main Doors and busily attaches a leafy bough to a Stage-Post, converting it immediately into a tree: while repeating the trick upon the other Post, she is interrupted by a robust voice: **How now spirit, whither wander you?** She is a spirit, it seems, not one of us mortals. She is, however, startled by a grinning figure, sitting in the middle of the Stage, and clearly pleased at having made her jump by his unobserved entry *at another* Door. The tripping rhythm of the Fairy's answer to this challenge is not disguised in the crowded lineation of Folio and Quartos, although it took the compositors a few lines to reconcile themselves to the new metres. The Fairy's opening words, in a pattern of rapid anapaests, rhythmically unique in the play, carry us irresistibly away from palace and carpenter's shop:

> **Over hill, over dale,**
> **Thorough bush, thorough briar,**
> **Over park, over pale,**
> **Thorough flood, thorough fire . . .**

The verse-pattern then settles down to a tetrameter couplet, a metrical scheme which Shakespeare reserves for the fairies' use—though they do not always use it. This rhythmical change gave much pleasure to Coleridge: 'The eight amphimacers have so delightful an effect on the ear! and then the sweet transition to the trochaic.' The Fairy puts us once more in mind of the moon, looking up at that quarter of the playhouse roof where we have learnt to expect it to shine:

I do wander every where,
Swifter than the Moon's sphere . . .

(and the monosyllable of 'Moon', prolonged to fill the measure of the line, is eloquent). She tells us her office as servant of the Fairy Queen and her function, **to dew her orbs upon the green**; and this she proceeds to do, for the orb, the circle, which she now sprinkles with dew is to be the Queen's dancing-ground for tonight. Typical of the subtlety of Shakespeare's versification in this play is the almost imperceptible slide in mid-couplet into the normal pentameter (the early compositors, of course, made no recognition of this change):

I must go seek some dew drops here,
And hang a pearl in every cowslip's ear.

We notice that, though her interlocutor is a spirit like herself, he is to her a **Lob of spirits.** The word suggests a clown or a lout: it is akin to 'lubber'. Master Slender, when cheated of his love by Mistress Page's trick of substitution, cries out: 'I came yonder at Eton to marry Mistress Anne Page, and she's a great lubberly boy' (THE MERRY WIVES OF WINDSOR, V.v.201 f.). But the best footnote to Shakespeare's conception of the 'Lob of spirits' is provided by Milton, writing more than a generation later: in *L'Allegro* (105 ff.) he speaks of

. . . how the drudging Goblin sweat,
To earn his Cream-bowl duly set,
When in one night, ere glimpse of morn,
His shadowy Flail hath thresh'd the Corn
That ten day-labourers could not end,
Then lies him down the Lubber Fiend,
And stretch'd out all the Chimney's length,
Basks at the fire his hairy strength;
And Crop-full out of doors he flings,
Ere the first Cock his Matin rings.

Just such a robust earthy spirit (the paradox is Shakespeare's) re-

[handwritten margin note: love in nature to the king & Queen & between them.]

sponds with a sharp warning of King Oberon's approach: he is **passing fell and wrath** with his Queen, and the bone of contention is **A lovely boy stol'n from an Indian King**. The atmosphere of the fairies' haunts is gradually but persistently built upon the foundations already laid in passing reference in the earlier scenes. At this point we have a vivid picture, anticipating what we are just about to see:

> **And now they never meet in grove, or green,**
> **By fountain clear, or spangled star-light sheen,**
> **But they do square, that all their Elves for fear**
> **Creep into Acorn cups and hide them there.**

The scale of life is being subtly diminished too.[9] The **Cowslips tall** are the Queen's pensioners: courtier-like, they wear a pearl ear-ring—but the pearl is a dewdrop. The terrified elves will **creep into Acorn cups** for safety. It is worth remarking that Shakespeare's poetical medium makes possible a transient flexibility in the presentation of the fairies' size: in one and the same scene Titania can wind Bottom in her arms and Peaseblossom can be sent to use his weapons in attacking the honey-bee; so too the elves who can be thought of as creeping, in their fear, into acorn-cups, are four-foot choristers.

Then—when our interest has already been kindled to expect a dramatic confrontation—and not till then, we are encouraged to speculate on the identity of the 'Lob of spirits'. He appears larger, broader and more 'lubberly' than the other attendant fairies; his **shape and making**, at any rate, are clearly different from theirs. The Fairy's guessing question does more than suggest the three evocative names of **Robin Good-fellow, Hobgoblin** and **Puck**; she describes his habits of mischief, mockery, menace and finally blackmail:

> **Those that Hobgoblin call you, and sweet Puck,**
> **You do their work, and they shall have good luck.**

The similarity to Milton's later description is plain, and it is noticeable that Shakespeare, like Milton, is projecting an image of country folk-lore, native to Warwickshire rather than to Greece,[10] and contrasting strangely with the 'Indian King' of whom Puck has just spoken: the contrast is to be developed more elaborately in the sequel and contributes largely to the verisimilitude of the fairy world. Puck's answer likewise deals with English country matters. As he illustrates with acrobatic mime the **Gossip's bowl** that bobs against her lip, the **three-foot stool** that slips from beneath the **wisest Aunt**, and the choir that **hold their hips, and laugh** at her discomfiture, he conjures up a whole series of pictures of village life for the enjoyment of the groundlings no less than the gallery audience. To the Fairy he is a somewhat formidable person, his own description is of a **merry wanderer of the night**: and he establishes his role in the play firmly as the King's Fool: **I jest to Oberon**. Music of fairy-voices approaching from a distance gives the alert, and both speakers retreat before the arrival of the King and Queen.

[60-117] We are carried straight back to Shakespeare's playhouse and the daring simplicity of his presentation by the stark directions of both Quarto and Folio: *Enter the King of Fairies, at one doore, with his traine; and the Queene, at another, with hers*. In practice, it seems likely that the Queen is on first, preceded by her court who prepare to dance in the orb which the Fairy attendant has so busily dewed upon the green: it is clear from Titania's invitation at *line* 140 that her purpose in coming to this spot was to dance a round; and Oberon's interruption provides the substance of her complaint, at *line* 86, that his 'brawls' have prevented them from dancing their 'ringlets to the whistling Wind'. The King's aggressive line puts an unexpected and unwelcome check upon their intention to dance:

Ill met by Moon-light, proud Titania.

It is an uncompromising challenge: we do not doubt, as his eye seeks the moon in the familiar quarter, that it is night in the wood, and Shakespeare's bold confidence is vindicated in the mind's eye. The opening exchange, immediately naming the protagonists, dramatises the contention for which Puck's vivid phrase, 'they do square', has prepared us:

Ill met by Moon-light, proud Titania.
—What, jealous Oberon? Fairy skip hence.
I have forsworn his bed and company.
—Tarry rash Wanton; am not I thy Lord?
—Then I must be thy Lady.

The stage movement is implicit in the dialogue. The Queen's train
are set for the beginning of their dance. The King's sinister salutation
startles them into immobility. Titania's order sends them in swift retreat towards the Door from which they entered. Oberon's 'Tarry'
halts their flight, and the two parties confront each other in defiant
opposition.

The first thing that the dramatist tells us about the Fairy King and
Queen is that each of them has a personal interest in the wedding of
Theseus and Hippolyta. This is developed in mock-heroic vein: the
slanderous accusation and counter-accusation, the *tu quoque* recrimina-
tion, the infatuated protection of the beloved mortal by the immortal
patron—these are themes as old as Homer's Olympians intervening at
Troy. The scale is miniature, but the reminiscence of the epic order is
palpable: the Sylphs of Pope's *Rape of the Lock* carry the parody a
stage farther: Shakespeare's Fairies are to be taken with a smaller pinch
of salt. Though Oberon's penchant for his **buskin'd Mistress** and
Titania's will o'the wisp enticement of Theseus **through the glimmering night** are quite forgotten in the sequel, their power and inclination to influence and control the life of mortals is immediately established, and the way is paved for the play's dénouement, when they
will come on the wedding-night **To give their bed joy and prosperity**. We notice in passing the strange mixture of associations with
which Shakespeare invests his fairy world: Greek legend and history
are represented not only by Theseus and Hippolyta but also by the
pastoral Corin and Phillida and the list of forlorn ladies whom Theseus
has betrayed: **Fairy Land**, however, is located at **the farthest steep
of India**, perhaps in a conscious attempt to evoke a sense of the
exotic.[11] The mixture is no doubt deliberate and helps to create the
atmosphere of magic and mystery. And it is injected in Titania's next
speech with a strong dose of native imagery, supporting, as Shakes-

peare's habit is, an exotic theme by relating it to every-day contemporary life. The audience might be townsmen, but London was small enough in those days to have the country within walking distance; and their personal experience would respond to the real and familiar dangers expressed in the evocation of the unseasonable weather and its disastrous effects—the **Contagious fogs**, the flood-water of **every pelting River** ruining the crops, so that the **Ploughman** has **lost his sweat**, the cattle are dying, and (most homely touches) **the nine men's Morris** (the squared diagram cut out of the turf for an open-air game of draughts) **is fill'd up with mud** and the **quaint Mazes** (the pitch for sports on the village-green) **are undistinguishable**. This long speech of Titania's, running to nearly forty lines, demands great skill of utterance from the boy-player. Charged throughout with resentful pathos, expressed in the unrhymed pentameters of debate, it has many incidental beauties of phrasing and imagery. The exquisite conceit of the **green Corn** that **Hath rotted, ere his youth attain'd a beard** reminds us that we are still in the period of Shakespeare's sonnet-writing, when he conceived of 'Summer's green all girded up in sheaves Borne on the bier with white and bristly beard' (Sonnet XII). Once again, and more vividly than ever, the presence of the moon is conjured up in the playhouse, as all the fairies, of both trains, stare in awe-struck wonder at the familiar quarter of the roof:

> **Therefore the Moon (the governess of floods)**
> **Pale in her anger, washes all the air;**
> **That Rheumatic diseases do abound.**

The alteration of the seasons is illustrated in two memorable paradoxes:

> **hoary headed frosts**
> **Fall in the fresh lap of the crimson Rose,**
> **And on old Hiems' thin and Icy crown,**
> **An odorous Chaplet of sweet Summer buds**
> **Is as in mockery set.**

Pathos and derision merge in the climax of indignation, hammered home in the rhetorical stress of **our . . . our . . . we . . .**:

> And this same progeny of evils comes
> From our debate, from our dissension:
> We are their Parents and original.

By the time she has finished, if the player has done his job well, we are far removed from the Duke's palace and the carpenter's shop. We are out in the wood, at night, in strange company: and our interest is focused on a dramatic quarrel which, in spite of the slight stature of its contestants, is enough to alter the course of nature and influence the fortunes of mortal men.

[118-145] The cause of the quarrel seems trivial enough: it is a squabble over the possession of **a little changeling boy**, but Shakespeare is at pains to give this cause some substance. Titania's account of the boy's origin and of the reason for her interest in him is elaborate both in motivation and in expression:

> His mother was a Vot'ress of my Order,
> And in the spiced Indian air, by night,
> Full often hath she gossip'd by my side . . .

Together they watched the merchant-ships out at sea, and as their sails grew **big-bellied with the wanton wind**, the Indian girl, already carrying the child in her womb, would gaily imitate the ships and **sail upon the Land**. Her **swimming gait** delighted her royal companion. It is a charming and affectionate picture. Then follows the pathetic conclusion of the story, told with utter simplicity, all conceit and extravagance eschewed:

> But she, being mortal, of that boy did die,
> And, for her sake, do I rear up her boy:
> And, for her sake, I will not part with him.

The punctuation here is that of the Fisher Quarto, and may represent Shakespeare's instructions to the boy-player. It is difficult to see why some critics speak of the fairies as heartless (Gervinus, for instance, says: 'He depicts them as beings without delicate feeling and without morality'). Oberon's leading question as to the Queen's immediate plans receives a suitably teasing answer: perhaps she may stay in this wood **till after Theseus' wedding day**. Her answer serves to point once again to the probable dénouement of the play: the overall structure is compact and shapely, and the end, though it may contain surprises, will seem on reflection to be inevitable. Meanwhile we too are content to stay **within this wood**.

[146-187] The Queen sweeps out in dignified defiance with her train, and the King, vowing to **torment** her **for this injury**, dismisses his followers: only his jester-servant is summoned to his side: **my gentle Puck come hither**. The familiar passage which follows, with its hardly disguised compliment to Queen Elizabeth, and its possible reminiscence of her famous visit to Kenilworth and the water-fête on the lake in the park, was clearly designed by Shakespeare for a particular audience on a particular occasion. But the lines are so written that they need no special knowledge of topical allusion to make a powerful effect on those 'sundry times' when the play was 'publickely acted'; and they fulfil their dramatic function in the structure of the play, which is to invest with magic the **little western flower** whose **juice . . .**

> . . . **on sleeping eye-lids laid,**
> **Will make or man or woman madly dote**
> **Upon the next live creature that it sees.**

Titania's departure has marked the end of the exposition of the play. The little flower, now so momentously introduced to us, is no mere property: by its magical agency the separate strands of the comedy will be woven together. In a different context, a similar passage of elaborate descriptive narration fulfils the same function of investing with magic an important property, a vital instrument in the play's plot, when Othello describes to Desdemona the handkerchief she has lost (OTHELLO, III.iv.56–76). Here the actor's task is to convey the substance of Oberon's tale to the mind's eye of his audience: with his gesture he points the geography of that strange landscape—fixing the **cold Moon** in its now habitual quarter; showing **Cupid all arm'd** aloft, above one side of the Stage; and the **fair Vestal, throned** on the other side; loosing the **love-shaft smartly**; then checking it in mid-flight as it is **quench'd** (the very sound of the word clogging the pace of the arrow) **in the chaste beams of the wat'ry Moon**; returning then with a glance to the undisturbed progress of **the imperial Vot'ress**; pointing then to the abrupt descent of **the bolt of Cupid**; seeing the **little western flower** directly at his feet; smiling ironically at the name which maidens call it, **Love in idleness**. The changing rhythm and tempo of the lines themselves give pace to Cupid's arrow and majesty to the Virgin Queen: and the imaginary motion-picture is clearly visible to the mind's eye, detached from Oberon's immediate surroundings on the unlocalised Stage of the playhouse. Puck's parting words are the poetical embodiment of his speed: the Quarto's slow, spread, capacious line of putting **a girdle, round about the earth** races away from the starting-gate with the galloping consonants of **in forty minutes**. Left alone, Oberon tells us what his purpose is, in a soliloquy at once informative and charged with a note of sinister gloating: there is relish in the catalogue of animals and in the sardonic contrast of **the soul of love**, and the climax is one of the conscious enjoyment of power:

I'll make her render up her Page to me.

the use/pretence of love to get your own way

He is interrupted by the sound of approaching footsteps, and when he assures us that he is **invisible** we do not doubt his word: his demeanour and that of the newcomers make it plain that he cannot be seen by mortal eye.

[188-246] *Enter Demetrius, Helena following him.* The robust timbre of Burbage's voice and his adult stature adjust our focus back to mortal scale. The story follows its expected course, explicitly stated (as Shakespeare's wont is) in the opening words: **I love thee not, therefore pursue me not**. We know at once that Helena has put her proposed plan into action: she has told Demetrius 'of fair Hermia's flight', and he has followed the eloping pair to the wood. The language is full of those conceits and verbal tricks which the Chamberlain's Men (and boys) were trained to make the most of—

> Where is Lysander, and fair Hermia?
> The one I'll slay, the other slayeth me . . .

and the quibble of **wood within this wood**; and the elaborate fancy of the **hard-hearted Adamant**:

> But yet you draw not Iron, for my heart
> Is true as steel.

Helena is both absurd and pathetic. She is absurd to us with her spaniel-fawning and the naïve echo to Demetrius's cruel rebuff:

> . . . I am sick when I do look on thee.
> —And I am sick when I look not on you.

But she is an object of concern to the gallant King of Fairies, whose invisible presence crosses the young man's path and whose countenance shows his sympathy with the lady's dismay. We are kept in mind of the wood and of Helena's danger by such phrases as

> To trust the opportunity of night,
> And the ill counsel of a desert place . . .

(the back-stage men no doubt contributing to the illusion with the well-timed hoot of an owl), and

> I'll run from thee, and hide me in the brakes,
> And leave thee to the mercy of wild beasts.

A tour-de-force of speech for the boy-actor is the running series of paradoxes,

> Apollo flies, and Daphne holds the chase;
> The Dove pursues the Griffin, the mild Hind
> Makes speed to catch the Tiger. Bootless speed,
> When cowardice pursues, and valour flies.

Great resilience of pitch was needed to project the emphasis of such a passage: it must be clear that Apollo (who should not fly) flies, that it should not be the dove but the griffin who pursues, that indeed in every instance of the series, **the story shall be chang'd.** This sort of vocal dexterity was presumably part of the grammar of the actor's schooling. Shakespeare would not write so, if his actors could not speak so. As Demetrius steals away, Helena falls into the rhyming couplets which mark a conclusion. When the pair have gone, Daphne still chasing her Apollo, Oberon catches up her device with a rhyming couplet of valediction; he catches up her phrase too in expressing his intention to intervene:

Thou shalt fly him, and he shall seek thy love.

The story, we observe, is being worked out in poetical terms.

[247-268]   Puck, returning out of breath, by the opposite Door to that by which he last went (for he has, after all, put a girdle round about the earth), presents the flower to his master. After a brief pause, while Oberon and the audience contemplate it, and the magic power evoked by his description of its strange history gathers again in the imagination, he embarks on a speech which has become famous in the anthologies and has on occasion been sung as a lyric to a musical setting. That is not Shakespeare's intention. The passage is both descriptive and informative, a necessary item in the course of the narrative: it begins with a line which is rhythmically matter-of-fact:

I know a bank where the wild thyme blows ...

Some editors have not resisted the temptation to emend 'where' to 'whereon', wishfully suiting their lyrical preconceptions. Shakespeare's actor, however, will not have sung or cooed these lines, for their function is different: they paint a picture (for the mind's eye of the audience) of Titania's sleeping-quarters, so that when, in the next moment, we see the familiar property moss-bank in the Study-space, decked no doubt for the afternoon with a more than usual abundance of flowers, we shall recognise it for the Queen's couch and invest it with all the detailed features of Oberon's description—**Oxlips and the nodding Violet,** a canopy of **luscious woodbine . . . sweet musk roses** and **Eglantine,** even with the **enamell'd skin** thrown there by the snake. Meanwhile, having repeated his intention to streak the sleeping Queen's eyes with the love-juice, Oberon commissions Puck to make other use of it, by applying it to the eyes of the **disdainful youth,** Demetrius, with whom **a sweet Athenian Lady is in love.** He is to **do it when the next thing he espies, May be the Lady:** and he is to report back **ere the first Cock crow.** While therefore the earlier part of the speech prepares us both atmospherically and factually for a scene which we shall soon witness, the second part is mainly informative, like those plot-furthering soliloquies with which from time to time Shakespeare kept his audience in touch with the progress of his story. It is not only Puck, but we too in the audience, who must listen carefully to the King's instructions.

*   *   *

[II.ii.1-26] No sooner have Oberon and Puck left the Stage, by opposite Doors, than the Study-curtains are opened, for the first time in the play, and disclose at one side of the discovery-space that 'bank where the wild thyme blows'. On the other side another item of property-furniture can likewise be deduced from the narrative needs of the play: it is the 'hawthorn brake' which will feature in III.i as 'tiring house' for the mechanicals' rehearsal. Once opened, the curtains will remain so till the story leaves the wood and returns to the town. The Queen of the Fairies is retiring to sleep: the ceremonial involves a dance (a **Roundel**) and a **Fairy song.** The Queen's train includes four Gentlemen, as we know from their subsequent encounters with Bottom, and the offices she assigns them are tasks of some difficulty and danger, to **kill Cankers in the musk rose buds,** to **war with Reremice, for their leathern wings,** to **keep back The clamorous Owl.** The song too is concerned with protecting the Queen's slumbers from the hostile intruders indigenous to the wood—**Snakes, Hedgehogs, Newts and blindworms, Spiders, Beetles** and **Snail.** Only the nightingale—**Philomel with melody**—is invited to assist in singing **our sweet Lullaby.**

Fairies sing. It seems likely that the first four lines of each stanza (the lines of prohibition) were sung to a single strain of melody, while the refrain, **Philomel with melody, &c.**, suggests the polyphonic weaving of the madrigal style. After the stage-direction, *Fairies sing*, the song in all the early texts is printed as a unit, and there is a speech-heading at the second stanza, **Weaving Spiders . . .** (in the Quartos, First Fairy; and in the Folio, Second Fairy). This certainly suggests a change of solo voice, while the repetition of the refrain suggests a chorus or 'burthen'. This combination of solo voice and chorus is not unknown in the plays (for instance, 'Come unto these yellow sands' from THE TEMPEST). Examples of lullabies of the time which follow the same verbal pattern and would respond well to the same musical treatment are Pilkington's 'Rest, Sweet Nymphs' and Peerson's 'Upon my lap my Sovereign sits'. The concluding couplet, **Hence away . . .**, is also printed as part of the lullaby, but both its dramatic purport and its position outside the strophic shape indicate that it is to be treated separately, perhaps as dialogue rather than song.

The gentle cadence is followed by a silence; then the whispered couplet from the first Fairy dismisses the singers:

> **Hence away, now all is well;**
> **One aloof, stand Sentinel.**

The lullaby has done its work; as the Folio direction has it, *Shee sleepes*. Peaseblossom, in flower-helmet and with iris-swordblade, is left pacing up and down before the Queen sleeping under her canopy of luscious woodbine. Both the tasks assigned by the Queen to her servants and the words of the lullaby create the atmosphere of a forest which is at once charmingly pastoral and full of dangers for the spirits who sleep and dance there; moreover we know already that there is a state of war in the wood. Now the sight of the pacing sentinel adds a final touch to this impression of hazards in the offing. The ground has been prepared for the violation of Titania's slumber.

[27-34] Out from behind the hawthorn-brake in the Study comes Oberon: he beckons to two of his braves who spring on the unsuspecting sentinel, disarm him and carry him, kicking but not screaming, off

stage. Then the King, more dangerous than any spotted snake, having the Queen at his mercy, squeezes the magic juice upon her eyelids, and utters his incantation:

What thou seest when thou dost wake,
Do it for thy true Love take:
Love and languish for his sake.

The rhyme-scheme is nicely contrived, for after the first triplet, the second group is extended to a fourth line:

When thou wak'st, it is thy dear . . .

and yet another extension comes then as a malicious afterthought:

Wake when some vile thing is near.

A further catalogue of animals (**be it Ounce, or Cat, or Bear . . .**) has already brought to mind Oberon's first conception of his plan. Now this postscript, reinforcing the sense of gloating relish, is calculated to make the audience laugh: and Oberon departs, leaving them wondering what that 'vile thing' will be.

[35–65] But the Queen and her danger are soon forgotten, for a new arrival absorbs our attention. Once again a voice of adult timbre overbears the slender tones of fairy speech. We recognise Lysander and Hermia, and remember their seven-league journey to the house of that 'Widow Aunt', that 'dowager, Of great revenue'. Now Hermia seems to **faint with wandering in the wood** and Lysander has to confess that he has forgotten the way. Their dialogue opens with an elegantly turned quatrain, rhyming alternately, and this continues the style of formal comedy which, in a different mood, the other pair also adopted. After the opening quatrain, the rest is in rhyming couplets, except when Hermia, commenting on the very elegance of Lysander's riddling, adds a third rhyme to the couplet of his smugly complacent cadence. He indeed **riddles very prettily**, for picking up the assonance of her

Nay good Lysander, for my sake my dear
Lie further off yet, do not lie so near . . .

he steers his syllogism to a witty conclusion:

**Then by your side, no bed-room me deny,
For lying so, Hermia, I do not lie.**

The triple pun (*Ly*sander and the two senses of 'lie') runs through the whole passage. It is an example of what Matthew Arnold called Shakespeare's 'overcuriousness of expression': but the literary critic will often be deaf to the playwright's art: here the quibbling is put to good dramatic effect; for the necessary question of this episode of the play is where the unexpectedly benighted lovers are to *lie* for their night's rest. The quibbling, besides giving pleasure to Hermia and Lysander, and to some of the judicious among their audience, throws the dramatic emphasis where the narrative demands it; the comedy of errors which is to ensue will spring from their present separation. Lysander consents to **lie further off**, and they settle down, one in front of each of the Stage-Posts, on their bed of rushes. The harmony of their relationship, so soon to be disrupted, is happily phrased in the rhymes of a divided couplet:

**Here is my bed: sleep give thee all his rest.
—With half that wish, the wisher's eyes be press'd.**

And, as if pointing the comic structure of the play, the Folio echoes its own direction of a moment before: *They sleepe.*

[66-83] Unexpected contrast in the demeanour of a character is one of the dramatist's most effective devices. Puck, who has recently girdled the earth in forty minutes, returns now to the Stage tired and foot-sore, kicking the rushes in boredom, all interest in his mission lost. He speaks in tetrameter verse, with rhyming pairs, and we can admire the variety of mood which Shakespeare can express in this seemingly restrictive metre: first the boredom of the frustrated mission—

Through the Forest have I gone,
But Athenian found I none . . .

then the startled exclamation—

Night and silence: who is here?

as he sees the sleeping figure of Lysander; then the amused satisfaction, as he finds the lady too—

And here the maiden sleeping sound,
On the dank and dirty ground . . .

and the sympathetic gallantry of his indignation at the fellow who, he thinks, does her wrong:

Pretty soul, she durst not lie
Near this lack-love, this kill-courtesy . . .

(the latter line swollen out to match its scornful sense); and last, the solemn voice of incantation as, trying a new experiment which promises some fun for the experimenter, he squeezes the juice on the lover's eyelids:

Churl, upon thy eyes I throw
All the power this charm doth owe . . .

When he hears the sound of hurried footsteps, he dives into the Trap-Door perhaps, his lively spirits restored, to find his way back to Oberon. By means of such an exit, we are given the sense that he vanishes suddenly before the presence of the approaching mortals; and while they occupy our attention, we feel that the ground itself is harbouring the mischievous spirit which is to bedevil them.

[84-134] There is charm in the coincidence that, while Helena and Demetrius have crossed Oberon's path, Hermia and Lysander have fortuitously crossed Puck's. And the coincidence does not stop there.

Enter Demetrius and Helena running. Four lines of rhyming stichomythia are enough to re-establish Helena's vain pursuit of Demetrius: he leaves her abruptly, he leaves her **darkling**, and her timid word reminds us of the danger of her situation. **Out of breath**, she leans for support against the trunk of a tree: it is the Stage-Post beneath which Hermia is sleeping. The irony of her unawareness is sharply pointed in her exclamation,

> **Happy is Hermia, wheresoe'er she lies . . .**

Shakespeare has written a note of absurdity into her part: she is the simpler-minded, the more naïve of the two girls, and her ineffectual ingenuousness is meant to make us smile:

> **No, no, I am as ugly as a Bear;**
> **For beasts that meet me, run away for fear.**

The artifice of rhyming couplets has also its comic development when reflective soliloquy turns to startled reaction: straying in her meditation towards the next tree (the other Stage-Post) she jumps out of her skin at sight of a recumbent figure:

> **But who is here? Lysander, on the ground?**
> **Dead, or asleep? I see no blood, no wound . . .**

Then this same artifice produces an irresistible touch of comedy, as Lysander, roused by a timid shaking of his shoulder, gazes ecstatically into her eyes. For the immediate and overwhelming effect of Puck's powerful charm is evidenced by Lysander's capping Helena's line with a clinching rhyme:

> **Lysander, if you live, good sir awake.**
> **—And run through fire I will for thy sweet sake.**

The effect of the drug is remarkable indeed: conceit becomes more extravagant than ever: Helena is **transparent**; he sees her heart through her bosom. Then threatening the rival Demetrius, and thereby alarming the devoted Helena, he seeks in a passionate but tortuous process of argument to explain to her, and to himself, the change in his allegiance. His juggling with **reason** (the word skilfully placed in so many different positions in the pentameter line, including the rhymed ending) is Shakespeare's way of representing Lysander's intoxication. It is perhaps worth quoting the stock comment of a literary editor upon this speech: Verity says: 'The speech is a specimen of the strained style, dealing in somewhat affected diction . . . and fanciful thoughts . . . which is not uncommon in Shakespeare's early works.' Such a verdict takes no account of the dramatist's intention nor of the effect of the speech when spoken in context in the playhouse. The actor's glassy stare and befuddled diction, and Helena's dismayed recoil before his pursuit, make a scene of high comedy:

> **The will of man is by his reason sway'd:**
> **And reason says you are the worthier Maid.**
> **Things growing are not ripe until their season;**
> **So I being young, till now ripe not to reason,**
> **And touching now the point of human skill,**
> **Reason becomes the Marshal to my will . . .**

love produces Comedy ✳

Helena's indignation, expressed in her vigorous iterations—**Is't not enough, is't not enough . . . That I did never, no nor never can . . . Good troth you do me wrong (good sooth you do)**—is the natural outcome of his importunacy; and her departing thrust defines, with a timely relevance characteristic of her author's composition, the current situation in his complex plot:

> **Oh that a Lady of one man refus'd,**
> **Should of another therefore be abus'd.**

[135-144] With his keen ear for the evocative power of sound-effects, it seems likely that Shakespeare made free use during this sequence of the owl's hoot, which the back-stage men were adept at imitating. (It may even have made a mocking echo to Helena's line

'In such disdainful manner, me to woo'.) The sound creates immediately the illusion of lonely panic in the wood at night. Lysander's transformation is indeed complete. Standing beside the sleeping Hermia, to whom so recently he bade an affectionate goodnight, he gives utterance to a sort of ecstasy of loathing, explaining for us his volte-face by analogies of surfeit and conversion: his drug-changed feelings express themselves in an assertion which is unmistakably vindictive:

> So thou, my surfeit, and my heresy,
> Of all be hated; but the most of me . . .

Puck's philtre is certainly efficacious, and our anticipation of further complications is not entirely in the mood of comedy.

[145-156] Hermia, at any rate, is not amused at her predicament, and the scene of her waking is played by the boy-actor with all the passion of a tragedian's role: how often does comedy depend upon an illusion of real distress! All that reminds us of the comic framework of the play is the conscious artifice—observed by both poet and player —of the rhyming couplet. Once again we are struck by the versatility of Shakespeare's use of verse-forms. The moment of nightmare before waking, the relief of the realisation that it was only a dream, the recounting of the dream to Lysander (his vindictiveness accentuated by the picture of his **smiling** at the serpent's **cruel prey**), the gradual awareness of his absence (**what, remov'd? . . . What, out of hearing, gone?**), the rising volume of her cries (**Alack where are you? speak an if you hear: Speak of all loves**), the listening silence (filled at last by the owl?) which precedes her **No?**—all these varieties of mood and volume and pace are included in the formal framework of the rhymed couplet. The balance between drama and comedy is thereby most skilfully sustained.

*   *   *

[III.i.1-77] The uncanny silence which swallows up the unanswered cry of the poor girl's panic departure is broken by hallooing from both sides of the Tiring-House, and we remember that the craftsmen have a rendezvous for their rehearsal in the wood. Again a murmur of pleased anticipation is audible in Yard and Galleries alike. The stage-direction of all the early texts in its simplicity roundly recognises that it is time for the comic turn: *Enter the Clownes*. Shakespeare is glad of this spontaneous reaction from his audience, and while we are in uncritically receptive mood, he strikes home with an outrageously daring confidence-trick of double bluff: **here's a marvellous convenient place for our rehearsal**, says Quince: **This green plot shall be our stage, this hawthorn brake our tiring house**. We have not time or inclination to reflect that this Stage has been transformed by the words and miming of his actors into a green plot,[12] and that it is the Tiring-House itself which contains, on one side of its Study-space, a property bush we can accept as a hawthorn-brake. As Quince sits down under a tree, his 'scrip' in his hands and a lantern at his elbow to read by, to the serious business of rehearsal, there is a predictable interruption. Quince's **What say'st thou, bully Bottom?** suggests the accumulated irritation of many such interruptions. Bottom, self-important as ever, is determined to raise an objection to the content of the play: **the Ladies cannot abide** the sight of Pyramus's suicidal sword. The general consternation is voiced by old Starveling in a deliciously absurd suggestion: **I believe we must leave the killing out, when all is done** (a happy ending for the star-crossed lovers?). But Bottom has come prepared with an answer to his own objection: he has **a device to make all well**; and the device is a means to his own self-aggrandisement: **a Prologue** is to **tell them, that I Pyramus am not Pyramus, but Bottom the Weaver**. When Quince agrees to write **such a Prologue . . . in eight and six**, even that suggestion must be capped: **No, make it two more: let it be written in eight and eight**. A further objection is raised by Snout: **Will not the Ladies be afear'd of the Lion?** and Starveling, chuckling with dry sarcasm, glances at little Snug, who has the lion's part, and who has already perhaps shown excessive nervousness of the terrors of the wood at night: **I fear it, I promise you**. Bottom again takes the lead in meeting the problem; first magnifying the difficulty, and then brushing aside the suggestion of **another Prologue** (which might spoil the effect of his own), he gives Snug a demonstration, a master-class in diplomacy, gripping his arms from behind and working them like a puppet's to suit the words (**Ladies, or fair Ladies, I would wish you, or I would request you . . .**), till he reaches a triumphant climax with **there indeed let him name his name, and tell them plainly he is Snug the joiner.** The uproarious laughter at Snug's expense—for Snug is their habitual butt—is good-humoured teasing, and the whole playhouse enjoys the company of this genial band of friends, so deeply absorbed in their unfamiliar task of putting a play together. It will meanwhile not escape the shrewder among the audience that the task is not unfamiliar to the actors themselves: the Chamberlain's Men are presenting in parody an illuminating picture of their daily morning occupation—to rehearse a play.

    But there is two hard things . . . says Quince, and proceeds to raise two fundamental problems of the art of illusion. Again Shakespeare is bluffing us, for when he poses the question of how **to bring the Moon-light into a chamber,** he is helping us to forget that ever since we arrived in the wood, we have felt (in the afternoon daylight) the presence of the moon. In solving this problem, Quince for once rejects Bottom's enthusiastic suggestion to **leave a casement of the great chamber window (where we play) open, and the Moon may shine in at the casement:** instead he adopts the expedient of a symbolical figure; putting his lantern into Starveling's hand, he foreshadows his subsequent performance: **. . . one must come in with a bush of thorns and a lanthorn, and say he comes to disfigure, or to present the person of Moon-shine.** It is not surprising that, even in this players' company, symbolism has been preferred to realistic lighting. Meanwhile a third possibility, Shakespeare's own method, of poetical evocation, does not occur to their minds. The Wall likewise (the second hard thing) is to be represented by a symbolical figure, and Bottom, appropriating Quince's idea, translates it in the person of his questioner, Snout: **Some man or other must present wall, and let him have some Plaster, or some Loam, or some roughcast about him, to signify wall . . .,** and Snout is shown in sketch how his spread fingers will stand for **that cranny** through which Pyramus and Thisbe are to whisper. There is, we see, to be a part for each of the craftsmen: and at the same time we are aware that each of them has a distinct personality in private life.

[77-125]   And so, the committee meeting over, the rehearsal proper
begins: **Come, sit down every mother's son, and rehearse your
parts.** Pyramus is to begin, and when he has spoken his speech, he
must **enter into that Brake**—the hawthorn-brake, which Quince has
identified for us, at one side of the Study-space—**and so every one
according to his cue.** It is at this precise moment that Shakespeare's
long-range purpose begins to show itself: for into the midst of the
group, as they sit all about the Stage, intent on their written 'parts' or
on the compelling spectacle of Bottom's histrionic talent in action,
up from the central Trap-Door springs Puck, invisible, of course, to
them, and scenting immediately an opportunity for more mischief.
He reminds us of what we have certainly forgotten during nearly two
hundred lines of dialogue, that Titania has all this while been plainly
visible, asleep on her property-bank in the Study:

**What hempen home-spuns have we swaggering here,
So near the Cradle of the Fairy Queen?**

and seeing that there is a play toward, he settles down to watch:

**I'll be an auditor,
An Actor too perhaps, if I see cause.**

Pyramus takes the stage, Thisbe is bidden to stand forth, and receives
his protestations of love. Bottom stumbles over a word and is sharply
corrected by the pedantic author; Kemp is allowed his old comic
routine of recoiling from his dearest Thisbe's **breath**; the departure
off-stage is managed by the crudest of gambits:

**But hark, a voice: stay thou but here awhile,
And by and by I will to thee appear.**

Then Puck's rhyming comment, as he follows Bottom into the brake
(a postscript to Pyramus's alternately-rhymed stanza)—

A stranger Pyramus, than e'er played here

—seems to be a direct bid for the laughter of the judicious: 'this is the oddest Pyramus you ever saw on this Stage.'[13] Flute, left alone in mid-stage, with his own special brand of naïvety (we remember his romantic hopes of Thisbe as 'a wand'ring Knight') asks **Must I speak now?** and at Quince's bidding gallops through his lines with none of Bottom's expansive bravura. Quince, the perfectionist, is so much offended by the garbling misnomer of **Ninny's tomb** (a point of articulation over which Flute proves in the end incorrigible) that for a moment he almost overlooks the greater absurdity: puzzling at his manuscript by the dim lantern (and thereby still sustaining the illusion of night in the London afternoon) he realises what is wrong, and cries with the impatience of outraged authorship: **why, you must not speak that yet; that you answer to Pyramus: you speak all your part at once, cues and all.** So we are absorbed in laughing at Flute at the moment when Bottom reappears from the brake, waved on as if with a magic wand by the conjuror Puck. The Quartos mark no entry, and the Folio editors seem to be bemused too, for they do not tell us till after *The Clownes all Exit* and Puck after them, that *Enter Piramus with the Asse head* (what a whiff of the back-stage property-store is conveyed to our senses by that precise identification, 'the Asse head'!). But the dialogue, as it is preserved, makes the sequence of the action clear at this moment of highly organised confusion: the organiser is Shakespeare, and (as his habit is) the drama is embodied in the spoken word. Pyramus's **cue is past**, and Flute, reacting with a gormless **O** to Quince's sharp rebuke, repeats the cue-line:

as true as truest horse, that yet would never tire.

The punctuation of both Quarto and Folio makes it clear that Bottom, although he knows his words, does not understand their sense. What Quince wrote was 'If I were, fair Thisbe, . . .' (that is, if I were as true, beautiful Thisbe, . . .) 'I were only thine'. What Bottom says is:

If I were fair, Thisbe, I were only thine.

This same joke, the dislocation of sense through mispointing, is more thoroughly explored in the lamentable comedy of the mechanicals' performance before the Duke, though there it is the nervous author himself, speaking the Prologue, who is at fault.

His fellow-actors are so deeply absorbed in their parts, and Quince in puzzling over this nonsensical re-pointing of his line, that there is a moment of delay before anyone looks at Bottom. Then Quince, raising his eyes from his scrip, gives tongue to his horror at what he sees. Puck conducts and creates the panic, chasing them one by one off-stage. His speech is a tour-de-force of vocal agility, closely matching the physical agility of his scattering chase. Here is a prime example of Shakespeare's power to embody action in words, to create even so violent a mood as this panic stampede by *verbal* means. It is to be noticed that he uses a strictly formal stanza shape—with rhyme-scheme of A B A B C C, breaking the normal pentameter rhythm only in the second line of the stanza. He uses patterned correspondence too, twice repeating in the same order the sequence of the **horse**, the **hound**, the **hog**, the **headless bear**, the **fire**. The final couplet of the stanza—

> **And neigh, and bark, and grunt, and roar, and burn,**
> **Like horse, hound, hog, bear, fire, at every turn**

—needs five sounds different in pitch and quality—a neigh, a bark, a grunt, a roar and some energetic rising inflection like the flame of fire —repeated in the words 'horse, hound, hog, bear, fire', so that we can be sure, when all is done, that it is the horse that neighs, the hound that barks, the hog that grunts, the bear that roars, and the fire that burns. The speech requires great vocal dexterity in the boy-player—and alas, in practice, his skill may well have been wasted, drowned in the laughter and applause which the situation itself evokes.

Snout has to return, perhaps to retrieve a lantern. His question to Bottom, **What do I see on thee?**, confirms Bottom's impression that his fellows are playing a trick on him: he is defiantly angry and un-consciously ironical: **What do you see? You see an Ass-head of your own, do you?** The irony—that, in spite of his own and his fellows' opinion of him, his Ass's head is a cap that fits only too well—

is too rich for one hearing only: it will be heard again and again in the sequel. Quince, stealing back on a similar errand, for in his panic flight he has abandoned his precious scrip, gives memorable expression to the strange event before our eyes:

Bless thee Bottom, bless thee; thou art translated.

[126-170] So Will Kemp has—or seems to have—the Stage to himself. But he is inhibited by the Ass-head which masks his features, and moreover Shakespeare is at pains to keep him well within the character which he has so carefully composed for him: indeed he shows us a new, and delightfully comic, facet of that character. For the invincible assurance of Nick Bottom the weaver is a little shaken, now that he is deprived of the audience of his admiring fellows: more than that, he is not even sure any longer of their respectful admiration; he suspects them of playing a trick on him, **to make an ass of me** (again the unconscious irony), **to fright me if they could**; and when he decides to **sing that they shall hear I am not afraid**, it seems very much like whistling in the dark to keep his own spirits up. His ditty is raucous, the imitation of bird-song in various pitch filtered through the mask (and inflections) of the Ass. As he walks up and down 'so near the Cradle of the Fairy Queen', Titania, recumbent on the moss-bank, whom we have seen so long with unseeing eyes, stirs in her sleep, rises to a sitting position, and utters her immortal line:

What Angel wakes me from my flow'ry bed?

Immortal, because the comedy of this *coup-de-théâtre* will bring the house down in any audience at any period of stage-history.[14] We have been prepared for the moment, by Oberon's incantation, by our own sight of the effect of the drug upon Lysander, by Puck's line reminding us that the clowns' rehearsal was close to the Queen's couch, by all the comic manipulation of coincidence: but, like many a good theatrical stroke, when it comes the sheer aptness and ingenuity of it take our breath away: it is the best kind of surprise which makes one say 'of course: it had to happen that way'. Bottom's second stanza introduces the old joke about the cuckoo—that 'word of fear, Unpleasing to the married ear'—and Kemp makes the most of that simple appeal to groundling humour with the repeated call of **Cuckoo** sounding through the hee-hawing lips of the Ass-mask. The crude sound, with its cruder associations, gives comic point to Titania's rapture (expressed, as counterpoint to Bottom's relentless prose, in lyrically regular pentameters):

> **I pray thee gentle mortal, sing again,**
> **Mine ear is much enamoured of thy note.**

She is no less **enthralled** to his **shape**, which we can see, with detached vision, as palpably monstrous: and the third object of her admiration is his wit, which is exemplified in a somewhat laboured jest about the incompatibility of **reason and love**: after which Kemp finds himself wryly reminding his claque of groundling fans: **Nay, I can gleek upon occasion.** Dramatic need, the necessary question of the play, demands that Bottom should seem cacophonous, ugly and stupid, and Shakespeare has so written the passage that the clown's confident assurance, now that he is alone, benighted, translated, has become tentative diffidence, as of a man unsure of himself away from his regular beat. His one desire is **to get out of this wood**, and he makes a sudden attempt to escape, but the Queen makes an equally sudden movement to intercept his stumbling flight: she encircles him and casts a spell on him so that he cannot move. Even in her protestations of rapture and love, she has never departed from the dignity of pentameter verse: now there is a new imperiousness in her rhymed prohibition:

Opposites attract

> **Out of this wood, do not desire to go:**
> **Thou shalt remain here, whether thou wilt or no.**
> **I am a spirit of no common rate:**
> **The Summer still doth tend upon my state,**
> **And I do love thee.**

The loved one must be given the full treatment of Fairyland, and the

incongruousness of the process is made verbally clear in her expressed
intention to

> **purge thy mortal grossness so,**
> **That thou shalt like an airy spirit go.**

Out from every quarter of the Stage—the Study, the two Doors, the
Trap-Door—spring her attendants, *foure Fairyes*, at her command. The
roll-call and the answers, in order of naming, no less than the appropriately illustrative costumes, identify these for our inspection:

Pease-blossom, Cobweb, Moth, and Mustard-seed.

[170-210]   For their mistress's commands, Shakespeare has found
a new device of versification. The list of instructions, ten lines long,
is a series of end-stopped verses, with iteration of a single rhyme: the
effect is magical, mesmeric (with the thrice-repeated 'eyes'), soporific,
a deliberate monotony, a luscious recipe for luxurious leisure:

> **Hop in his walks, and gambol in his eyes,**
> **Feed him with Apricocks, and Dewberries,**
> **With purple Grapes, green Figs, and Mulberries,**
> **The honey-bags steal from the humble Bees,**
> **And for night-tapers crop their waxen thighs,**
> **And light them at the fiery Glow-worms' eyes,**
> **To have my love to bed, and to arise:**
> **And pluck the wings from painted Butterflies,**
> **To fan the Moon-beams from his sleeping eyes.**
> **Nod to him Elves, and do him courtesies.**

Bottom hardly rises to the occasion. His lumbering jokes are in deliberate contrast to the delicacy of Titania's imagery. They help to
give identity to the fairy attendants, who are nervous in approaching
the monster and bewildered by his sallies of wit: Cobweb for a cut
finger, Squash and Peascod as the parentage of Peaseblossom, the
kindred of Master Mustardseed that **hath made my eyes water ere**

now—these are frigid jests enough. Titania, besottedly unaware of the bathos, closes the scene with an elegant stanza which once more brings the presence of the moon into the playhouse: this time, however, as representative of the virgin Diana, she is noticed to be weeping (with **every little flower**) at the violation of chastity. It is an explicitly amorous cadence—interrupted, though, by an untimely bray from within the Ass-head, which elicits from the doting Queen an unplanned postscript, an extra rhyming line beyond the formal shape of the quatrain:

Tie up my lover's tongue, bring him silently.

A truss of hay is the appropriate means of sealing those hairy lips.

*   *   *

[III.ii.1-40]　　The story proceeds on its expected course. Titania has ushered her lover out in elegant procession through the Study behind her moss-bank. Not one of the early texts marks at this point a new scene; performance in the Elizabethan playhouse reflects this unbroken continuity, and with it the comic irony conveyed by the instant juxtaposition of these two episodes. Hard upon Titania's *Exit*, the Folio prints simply *Enter King of Pharies, solus.* Oberon emerges from one of the Doors on to the Stage itself, wondering

if Titania be awak'd;
Then what it was that next came in her eye,
Which she must dote on, in extremity.

He has not long to wait for his answer, for his messenger is near at hand, and his impatient question,

What night-rule now about this haunted grove?

keeps our imagination deeply immersed in the supernatural climate of the fairies' world. Puck's next task is yet another test of the player's histrionic skill. Shakespeare employs the device, which he has used before and will use again to good effect, of reproducing in the speech and mime of a narrator a scene which we have just witnessed in action: the Elizabethan Stage, with its clear-cut geometrical shape and its flexibility of localisation, by which it may at one time specify place and at another have no locality at all, is the ideal setting for such reconstructive narration. It is a device especially suited to the poetic drama, and one of the most profitable advantages of the medium: it differs from the Messenger-speeches of Greek tragedy in that we have already seen what the speaker describes; his own individual interpretation of what we have seen is the gratuitous bonus, and the audience have double value from the dramatic material thus repeated.[15] Puck now can describe to his master his latest exploit with mimicry of movement and gesture to recall every detail of the scene. He indicates the position of the Queen's **close and consecrated bower,** and introduces the **rude Mechanicals**; dispatches Pyramus into his **brake**; fixes the **Ass's nole** on his head; struts out of the bush (**And forth my Mimic comes**). Then the versatile player conjures before our eyes the detail of an elaborate simile—the **creeping Fowler,** the **gun's report** (duly represented with a clap of the hands), and the broad wheeling spread of his arms as the frightened birds **Sever themselves, and madly sweep the sky.** Then, back from the simile, he returns to the factual description of the mechanicals' stampede; indicating how **at our stamp** (he stamps his foot on the hollow stage) **here o'er and o'er one falls**; next impersonating that other **He** who **murther cries**; miming the prickly transit through the **briars and thorns** which **at their apparel snatch**; clearing the Stage for the dénouement which he himself has contrived, showing us, with the quizzical eye of the director, how he

> **. . . left sweet Pyramus translated there:**

and winding up his narrative with a calculated ambiguity—was it an accident, 'so near the Cradle of our Fairy Queen'?—and a sense of timing which reserves his climax to the very last word:

When in that moment (so it came to pass)
Titania wak'd, and straightway lov'd an Ass.

And so our memory of what has been enacted on the bare Stage is
heightened in colour, and we shall feel that we have seen not only the
terror of the mechanicals but the thorns and briars of the dark wood
which intensified that terror: we have been involved through hind-
sight in their discomfiture.

Oberon, who has supported Puck's mime with the growing interest
of his attentive eye, is delighted at the outcome:

This falls out better than I could devise . . .

which leaves the ambiguity still open: Puck may be a better contriver
than his master, but it will not be acknowledged; what about that
other task?

. . . hast thou yet latch'd the Athenian's eyes,
With the love juice . . . ?

Yes, **that is finish'd too**: and the woman was sleeping beside him,
so that **when he wak'd, of force she must be ey'd**. Again we must
admire the swift economy and insistent relevance of Shakespeare's
dramatic construction: for at this moment he brings on Demetrius and
Hermia, and the comic confusion is immediately defined in two
speeches, Oberon's

Stand close, this is the same Athenian

—and Puck's

This is the woman, but not this the man.

King and jester retire behind the hawthorn-brake in the Study, and
the mortals take the Stage.

[41-81] For more than four hundred lines in the sequel, the quartet of young Athenians and their affairs occupy the scene. It is an appropriate moment to reflect what impression each has made upon us so far. Helena is the taller of the girls, pathetic because she has been jilted, but more absurd in her helplessness than pitiable, abject in her fawning pursuit of her faithless lover, a little prudish in the manner of her rejection of Lysander's unexpected wooing. Hermia is the shorter one, dark of hair and complexion; this detail would of course be visible in the playhouse: it is the basis of Lysander's comment as he leaves her for Helena, 'Who will not change a Raven for a Dove?'; both her dark complexion and her short stature will be theatrically important in the sequel. She is obstinate in her defiance of her father's wish, steadfast in trial before the Duke, composed in the assurance of her lover's faith, understandably panic-stricken at finding herself alone in the wood but determined still in her desperation and never doubting his constancy ('Either death or you I'll find immediately'), altogether a much more positive person than her ineffectual friend. Our feelings about the two young men are prompted largely by their situation: Demetrius, the unwelcome suitor of Hermia, her father's choice (like Silvia's unwanted Thurio, or Juliet's Paris), once at least the butt of his rival's wit ('You have her father's love, Demetrius: Let me have Hermia's: do you marry him'), is early exposed as a 'spotted and inconstant man' and more recently presented as the most ungallant, indeed brutal spurner of his jilted lady's advances; Lysander we have found light of tongue, hopeful of heart, lyrical in his exposition of the course of true love, resourceful in planning and executing elopement, gracefully riddling in his choice of bed-room in the wood; and if subsequently he has appeared unnecessarily vindictive in the ecstasy of his loathing for his first love, we readily recognise that the man is not himself, under the influence of Oberon's transforming drug. So far, in fact, we like Lysander, and not even the well-graced person of Burbage has made us feel affection or admiration for Demetrius. Such are the members of the quartet whose conflicting passions sustain the high comedy of the ensuing imbroglio.

There is at once a piquant contrast in Demetrius's new demeanour: when last seen, he was rejecting the advances of his faithful love; now he is himself rejected. Hermia is characteristically **bitter** in her chiding, and is ready to curse him for killing Lysander in his sleep. Offering her heart, she bids him **kill me too**, and the drama of her desperate defiance stops for a moment the fluent regularity of her rhymed rhetoric: the words **and kill me too**, though squeezed in at the end of the line, in both Quarto and Folio, are *extra metrum*, after the rhyming word **deepe**. She cannot believe that her lover could **have stolen away, From sleeping Hermia**, and her sense of the improbability is expressed in a far-fetched analogy which once again draws inspiration from the continuing presence of the moon in the angle of the playhouse-roof:

> **I'll believe as soon**
> **This whole earth may be bor'd, and that the Moon**
> **May through the Centre creep, and so displease**
> **Her brother's noontide, with th'Antipodes.**

[margin handwritten: loyalty & faith in Lysa]

Demetrius, comparing Hermia's radiance to **yonder Venus in her glimmering sphere**, singles out with his glance another quarter of the night-sky above the wood. He denies that he is **guilty of Lysander's blood**, and the sparring is sharpened to a climax in rhymed stichomythia:

> **—Nor is he dead for aught that I can tell.**
> **—I pray thee tell me then that he is well.**
> **—And if I could, what should I get therefore?**
> **—A privilege, never to see me more.**

The comma of the early texts, after 'privilege', reveals how the boy-player was instructed to lead the suitor on—and then savagely disappoint his hopes.

[82-121]   As Demetrius, deciding that **there is no following her in this fierce vein**, settles down to sleep off **sorrow's heaviness**, Oberon comes forward from his concealment in the hawthorn-brake, and expresses his anxious indignation at Puck's mistake: clearly his plan has gone wrong, some true love has been infected with the love-juice:

> Of thy misprision, must perforce ensue
> Some true love turn'd, and not a false turn'd true.

That 'true love' we know is Lysander; and we remember his own
melancholy awareness that 'the course of true love never did run
smooth'. Meanwhile Puck is sent on a new errand:

> About the wood, go swifter than the wind,
> And Helena of Athens look thou find.

Oberon's picture of her present state is typical of the portrait we already
have of her:

> All fancy sick she is, and pale of cheer,
> With sighs of love, that costs the fresh blood dear.

Again Puck's speed, as he sets off on his mission, is embodied in the
movement of his verse—a slow line first, by way of a launching-pad,
the long O-syllables prolonged to swell the short measure of the pentameter; then the racing flight of the second line, which carries him off-
stage:

> I go, I go, look how I go,
> Swifter than arrow from the Tartar's bow.

Again for the application of the love-juice, Oberon uses the incantatory
tetrameter, and each one of the eight lines has the same mesmeric
rhyme. We are reminded of the magical origin of the charm, when
Cupid's bolt fell upon the little western flower:

> Flower of this purple dye,
> Hit with Cupid's archery,
> Sink in apple of his eye . . .

and Helena's anticipated appearance, when the sleeper awakes, is
compared in its glorious shining to **the Venus of the sky**, the planet

which was so recently conjured up in our imagination by Demetrius himself.

Puck's speed has indeed outflown the Tartar's arrow. Back he comes, promising the arrival of Helena

And the youth, mistook by me . . .

It is Lysander, of course; and he is still as before

Pleading for a Lover's fee.

Puck's couplet spreads to three lines—

Shall we their fond Pageant see?

and, irrepressibly in his infectious enjoyment, to a fourth rhyme:

Lord, what fools these mortals be!

We are already agog to relish the development of the tangle, and Shakespeare this time prepares us for the shape of things to come: Oberon points out that

> **the noise they make,**
> **Will cause Demetrius to awake.**

And Puck's comment sets a lighted match to the kindling of our anticipation:

> **Then will two at once woo one,**
> **That must needs be sport alone:**
> **And those things do best please me,**
> **That befall preposterously.**

The King's jester has become Shakespeare's interpreter: while Puck enjoys the preposterous confusion of these foolish mortals, we too know that we need not take the ensuing quarrel, however violent, too seriously. Puck's interpretative nouns shape our response: the entanglement, which in other circumstances would seem tragic, is no more than 'sport' or a 'Pageant'.

[122-176]   The long quarrel-scene, sustained throughout its length with unflagging ingenuity, makes full use of the wide and deep dimensions of the Stage, with its two Stage-Post trees for hiding or protection and its latitude for conspiratorially detached grouping and high-speed all-out chase and retreat. It begins formally: Lysander, for all his tears, preserves a shapely stanza of six (A B A B C C), and Helena, in spite of her vigorous rebuttal, is at pains to repeat the pattern. This formal verse-shape, a quatrain followed by a clinching couplet, seems to have been a favourite metrical device of Shakespeare's. A striking example of its dramatic use can be found in RICHARD II, III.ii.76–81. It is the stanza in which the narrative of VENUS AND ADONIS is told. The versification is deliberate, as Shakespeare works towards his next theatrical stroke: after the two matching stanzas, the dialogue continues in rhyming stichomythia:

> —I had no judgement, when to her I swore.
> —Nor none in my mind, now you give her o'er.
> —Demetrius loves her, and he loves not you.

Inevitably the ear expects a rhyme to 'you'. Instead we are startled by a voice from the ground: Demetrius himself, with Lysander's line still ringing in his (and our) ears, interrupts the flow of the rhymes with a new couplet of his own:

> O Helen, goddess, nymph, perfect, divine,
> To what, my love, shall I compare thine eyne?

The unexpected breaking of the rhyme-scheme echoes the unexpected reversal in sense, as Demetrius's protestation of love instantly belies Lysander's words. It is a most skilful comic device, and it will be noticed that Shakespeare takes a course exactly opposite to his likewise comic formula for the waking of Lysander, who was given a capping rhyme.* The outrageous clichés of Demetrius's love-talk make no appeal to Helena: indeed when he speaks of the temptation of her lips —**those kissing cherries**—she holds up a protesting hand, and when he attempts to fasten on that hand, which reduces the whiteness of **high Taurus' snow** to the colour of a crow, she slaps him smartly and breaks out into an outcry against both her suitors: she is not going to be taken in by their advances; she sees mockery in the extravagant imagery with which Shakespeare once more represents the effect of the drug:

> **If you were men, as men you are in show,**
> **You would not use a gentle Lady so;**
> **To vow, and swear, and superpraise my parts,**
> **When I am sure you hate me with your hearts.**

Refusing to take their courtship seriously, she interjects a third rhyme to Lysander's neat couplet of protestation:

> **And yours of Helena, to me bequeath,**
> **Whom I do love, and will do till my death.**
> **—Never did mockers waste more idle breath.**

But there they are, the pair of them, both kneeling at Helena's feet, each yielding up his interest in Hermia to the other—when Demetrius, who has the advantage of seeing the distant Door behind Lysander's back, scores a point over his rival, anticipating with relish his embarrassment:

> **Look where thy Love comes, yonder is thy dear.**

[177-344] Hermia's opening lines cover the outcome of her tentative searching for her lover through the trees: it is typical of Shakespeare's art that he embodies in words the girl's situation, as she escapes at last from her ordeal of groping through the wood:

* See *page 69, above.*

88

> Dark night, that from the eye his function takes,
> The ear more quick of apprehension makes;
> Wherein it doth impair the seeing sense,
> It pays the hearing double recompense.

Lysander is now in the position which we once particularly associated with Demetrius ('I'll run from thee, and hide me in the brakes'). It is now Lysander who, lurking behind a Stage-Post, is caught and must face the question **why unkindly didst thou leave me so?** There is only one answer; **Lysander's love** is **Fair Helena**:

> Could not this make thee know,
> The hate I bare thee, made me leave thee so?

The upshot of this revelation is delightfully funny, in spite of Hermia's genuine dismay: she cannot believe her ears; she is almost dumbstruck:

> You speak not as you think; it cannot be.

What makes us laugh is the sudden and unexpected interruption of Helena, triumphantly sure that she is right in her suspicion, and wrong again as usual:

> Lo, she is one of this confederacy.

Again the rhyme clinches the comic effect, and as if to ram the point home of the absurdity of the poor girl's slow-witted and mistaken realisation, Shakespeare gives her two more lines with the same rhyme:

> Now I perceive they have conjoin'd all three,
> To fashion this false sport in spite of me.

After that, the rhymes disappear and blank verse gives a more naturalistic treatment of the emotional storms of the quarrel. Helena's volubility is quite of a piece with her character as we have observed it, and the pace of her tirade leaves the other three speechless. The poet has been at pains to give us a sense of the past shared by the two girls, the old days of lying upon faint primrose beds in the wood, emptying their bosoms of their counsel sweet (I.i. 214 ff.). Now she draws Hermia down to sit beside her, and her enthusiastic recollection of **schooldays friendship, childhood innocence** breeds little explanatory gestures to show how with their needles the two girls

> **created both one flower,**
> **Both on one sampler, sitting on one cushion**

—and to illuminate the charming comparison of

> **a double cherry, seeming parted,**
> **But yet an union in partition,**
> **Two lovely berries moulded on one stem.**

Her memory of their shared childhood brings out all that is most feminine in her: she reproaches Hermia for joining forces with the enemy, **men**, for not being **maidenly**, for betraying not only Helena but all **our sex**. As she warms under pressure of her indignation, her **passionate words** are vigorous and pungent: there is something near wit in her phrase **your other love, Demetrius**, and satire in her catalogue of his words of praise,

> **To call me goddess, nymph, divine, and rare,**
> **Precious, celestial . . .**

But in the end her indignation (characteristically) evaporates into grizzling; sarcasm subsides into self-pity: we cannot help liking her, but neither can we help laughing at her:

> **What though I be not so in grace as you,**
> **So hung upon with love,**

(there is a barb in this phrase)

> so fortunate?
> (But miserable most, to love unlov'd)
> This you should pity, rather than despise.

As Hermia appeals in bewilderment to the others, they make for the moment a group at the front of the Stage: Helena has retreated from them in her misery, and turning now she thinks (again mistakenly) that they are putting their heads together in conspiracy:

> Ay, do, persever, counterfeit sad looks,
> Make mouths upon me when I turn my back,
> Wink each at other, hold the sweet jest up.

The action is written into the text, or implied in it: this is the essence of the poetic drama. That the three are at this moment very far from being in collusion, only makes Helena's misinterpretation of their accidentally close grouping the funnier. And funnier still is her grand gesture of departure:

> But fare ye well, 'tis partly mine own fault,
> Which death or absence soon shall remedy.

The pathetic bathos of the less drastic alternative to death is underlined by the fact that she does not after all depart.

While the creative imagination of the poet constantly gives verbal substance to the conflicting emotions of his quartet, the technique of his versification is no less powerfully resourceful in preserving the interest and tension of the scene. Sometimes he employs the hackneyed chiasmus:

> If she cannot entreat, I can compel.
> —Thou canst compel, no more than she entreat.

Sometimes he imports an occasional rhyme into the texture of his blank verse to accentuate a riposte:

> **I say, I love thee more than he can do.**
> **—If thou say so, withdraw and prove it too.**

Sometimes he breaks a line in two:

> **Quick, come.**
> **—Lysander, whereto tends all this?**

Throughout, the poet's inventive ear is changing the tune and for ever sustaining the long-running rhythm of the dialogue. Hermia throws herself between the sparring gallants, giving Demetrius the chance to mock Lysander as **a tame man.** The infuriated Lysander utters all manner of abuse to be rid of her: her dark complexion (unfashionable at Queen Elizabeth's court) makes her an **Ethiope**, a **tawny Tartar**; her clinging to her reluctant lover is vividly projected in the images of his cry, **Hang off thou cat, thou burr.** Hermia's final appeal has a tragic intensity, free of all conscious artifice:

> **What, can you do me greater harm than hate?**
> **Hate me, wherefore? O me, what news my Love?**
> **Am not I Hermia? Are not you Lysander?**
> **I am as fair now, as I was ere while.**
> **Since night you lov'd me; yet since night you left me.**
> **Why then you left me (O the gods forbid)**
> **In earnest, shall I say?**

The contrast with the stylistic elaboration of what has gone before is remarkable: it is as if Shakespeare was forbidding his audience to laugh at Hermia, as they had at Helena. The pathos of her situation is sharpened by Lysander's gunfire answer, with its cruel series of emphatic assertions, leading to uncompromising statement:

> **Therefore be out of hope, of question, of doubt;**
> **Be certain, nothing truer: 'tis no jest,**
> **That I do hate thee, and love Helena.**

And if her very next speech, with its sudden change of the angle of attack, makes us laugh indeed, it is more at the discomfiture of Helena's retreating figure than at Hermia's splendidly menacing aggressiveness:

O me, you juggler, you canker blossom . . .

This turning of the tables, after Helena's earlier tirade, is irresistibly comic. Hermia, who has suffered enough at Lysander's hands, now lets herself go upon what she thinks is an easier prey: it seems indeed at first an unequal contest, but Helena's characteristic charge that Hermia lacks **maiden shame**, and her hypocritical reference to her own **gentle tongue**, indicates that she is not as helpless as she seems. Nevertheless poor Helena all unconsciously provides her adversary with ammunition: for still believing that Hermia is in conspiracy against her, she calls her **counterfeit** and then paraphrases the word by another—**you puppet, you**. To play with words, to 'mistake the word', is an 'old vice' with Shakespeare, as one of his earliest clowns declares (Two GENTLEMEN OF VERONA, III.i.285). Hermia here mistakes the word 'puppet' and breeds from it a whole generation of comic invective:

Puppet? why so? Ay, that way goes the game.
Now I perceive that she hath made compare
Between our statures, she hath urg'd her height,
And with her personage, her tall personage,
Her height (forsooth) she hath prevail'd with him.

The cumulative effect of the repetitions is urgent and mounting, and is continued with an equally urgent iteration of **low (How low am I . . . How low am I?)**, slammed home with the gloriously apt caricature of the tall, gawky Helena:

How low am I, thou painted May-pole? Speak,
How low am I? I am not yet so low,
But that my nails can reach unto thine eyes.

There is room for Hermia to run on this broad Stage, room too for Helena to retreat. Protected by the strong arms of both her admirers, the modest maiden sustains a rearguard action of some skill. Under the guise of naïve self-deprecation she gibes at her rival, smugly emphasising the first-person pronoun:

> **I was never curst:**
> **I have no gift at all in shrewishness.**

She deliberately strikes at Hermia's weakest spot:

> **you perhaps may think,**
> **Because she is something lower than my self,**
> **That I can match her.**

She tries to argue with Hermia, to plead with her: and again the calculatedly histrionic gesture of renunciation falls flat before the brutal snub of her rival:

> **And now, so you will let me quiet go,**
> **To Athens will I bear my folly back,**
> **And follow you no further. Let me go.**
> **You see how simple, and how fond I am.**
> **—Why get you gone: who is't that hinders you?**

And the simple, fond girl cannot resist revealing a feature of her friend's character which casts a lurid light upon that 'schooldays friendship' earlier invoked in rosier tints:

> **O when she's angry, she is keen and shrewd,**
> **She was a vixen when she went to school,**
> **And though she be but little, she is fierce.**

Little again? cries Hermia, **Nothing but low and little?** (the iteration has reached a climax) . . . **Let me come to her**; and Lysander, in throwing her off, gives a new sharpness to the stigma of her stature:

> **Get you gone you dwarf,**
> **You minimus, of hind'ring knot-grass made,**
> **You bead, you acorn.**

Free of his encumbrance, he is at liberty to accept Demetrius's challenge, and the martial stalk of the rivals, marching off stage **cheek by jowl**, raises the plaudits of the whole playhouse as the climax of a scene of sustained brilliance. This is a little hard on the two boy-players, who have after all made the running, and who are now left stranded while the applause takes its time to subside. Shakespeare has thought of a device to meet this practical difficulty: their exit is contrived in terms of a chase. When she can make herself heard, Hermia advances upon her quarry. **Nay, go not back** has all the menace of the vixen that she was in her schooldays. There is the width of the Stage between the two, and Helena makes use of a Stage-Post, a tree, to dodge her assailant. Shakespeare eases the task of the boy-player by casting his exit-lines in rhyme. Helena is to win the last trick by a final sneer at her rival's stature and by her own high-stepping flight, the farthingale hitched well above the knees; and the action is again embodied in the words the poet puts into her mouth:

> **Your hands than mine, are quicker for a fray,**
> **My legs are longer though to run away.**

Once more the playhouse bursts into applause, and it is the positive, aggressive little puppet Hermia who is left alone without resource, and whose helpless, tongue-tied line epitomises the pass her brave adventure of elopement has brought her to:

> **I am amaz'd, and know not what to say.**

It is interesting to note that Hermia's exit-line, which is given in both the Quartos, is omitted from the Folio text. Perhaps Heminges and

Condell are recording the revolt of a succession of Hermias against the anticlimax of uttering this helpless admission of defeat. The whole long quarrel is an exhilarating sequence of high comedy, and the two boy-players, whose strength is in their tongues rather than in any feminine charm, have made the most of it. For once, the seasoned actors (Burbage himself and Condell) have been content to play a secondary role in support of their brilliant apprentices.

[345-377] Oberon and Puck emerge again from their conceal-ment within the Study, and Puck's respectful address to the **King of shadows** re-establishes the element of the supernatural, present in their persons throughout the quarrel, but entirely forgotten in the vigour and pace of the episode. Oberon is angry and threatening: it may be **negligence**, or it may be wilful knavery. Puck is momentarily apprehensive, but soon justifies himself and confesses that he is un-repentant:

> ... so far am I glad, it so did sort,
> As this their jangling I esteem a sport.

His word 'sport' has echoed through the scene: he anticipated the confusion so, before it began, and he describes it so at its end; and ironically it was the word used more than once by Helena in her anger to describe the importunate wooing of her lovers. But Puck's master, with a king's responsibility, decides that the sport has gone far enough. He bids Robin **overcast the night**. Although the greater part of the action of the play takes place at night, and we are never entirely allowed to forget it, Shakespeare uses his fullest powers of evocation to emphasise certain moments of his story, of which this is one. The fact of darkness has not been in the forefront of our minds since Hermia's entrance in the previous scene. Now it is necessary both to re-establish the natural darkness of the night and to intensify it by magical conjuration:

> The starry Welkin cover thou anon,
> With drooping fog as black as Acheron.

Puck's commission is one after his own heart:

> **Like to Lysander, sometime frame thy tongue,**
> **Then stir Demetrius up with bitter wrong;**
> **And sometime rail thou like Demetrius . . .**

The pugnacious lovers are to be led different ways until they abandon
their pursuit of each other and fall asleep. Sleep too, like darkness, is
evoked in especially powerful imagery:

> **Till o'er their brows, death-counterfeiting, sleep**
> **With leaden legs, and Batty-wings doth creep.**

Then **this herb** (an antidote) is to be crushed into Lysander's eye to

> **. . . make his eye-balls roll with wonted sight.**

Meanwhile the all-wise and now benevolent King of Fairies begins
to prepare us for a quiet resolution to all the disturbance: his healing
phrases put the confused adventures of this night in the wood into a
new perspective, recalling the play's title and the implicit promise of
the opening scene (I.i.8) that we should 'dream away the time' until
the Duke's wedding-day:

> **When they next wake, all this derision**
> **Shall seem a dream, and fruitless vision,**

(and appropriately there is to be a happy ending)

> **And back to Athens shall the Lovers wend**
> **With league, whose date till death shall never end.**

restoration
of
love .

The Queen too is included in the general amnesty,

> **. . . and all things shall be peace.**

[378-395] The dignified rhythmical monotony of the King's speech ends in a deliberately quiet cadence. The startling contrast of Puck's urgent interruption is equally deliberate:

> **My Fairy Lord, this must be done with haste,**
> **For night's swift Dragons cut the Clouds full fast,**
> **And yonder shines Aurora's harbinger.**

It is the first sign of the coming of dawn, and Puck sees 'Aurora's harbinger' (the morning star) in the opposite angle of the playhouse roof to that which we have so long associated with the moon. The evocation of the night passes to a new stage in this speech of Puck' and in Oberon's reply. It is the moment of transition, from night to day. The approach of daylight spells panic to Puck, and he curdles our blood a little with his grisly picture of how **Ghosts wand'ring here and there, Troop home to Church-yards**, and excites our pity for the **damned spirits** who

> **. . . wilfully themselves exile from light,**
> **And must for aye consort with black brow'd night.**

This is not a gratuitous digression: at this moment of urgency in the narrative Shakespeare deliberately takes time to create in the images of terror and damnation the darkest hour before dawn. Just as deliberately Oberon's reply creates in poetic terms the radiance which will dispel this darkness. He begins with an echo of Titania's 'I am a spirit of no common rate', and a hint of the royal prerogative in cheerfully amorous dalliance as the red sun rises:

> **But we are spirits of another sort:**
> **I, with the morning's love have oft made sport,**
> **And like a Forester, the groves may tread,**
> **Even till the Eastern gate all fiery red,**

(at the words Puck faces east, looking towards Aurora's harbinger, and

immediately shields his eyes with his arm from the imagined glare of
Oberon's prediction)

> **Opening on Neptune, with fair blessed beams,**
> **Turns into yellow gold, his salt green streams.**

And with these 'fair blessed beams' the disturbing thought of Puck's
'damned spirits' has been exorcised. After the transition thus engineered,
the urgency of the situation, first heralded by Puck, must be re-
created:

> **But notwithstanding, haste, make no delay:**
> **We may effect this business, yet ere day.**

The promised sunrise has not yet come to the playhouse.

[396-464]   With this sense of urgency, and the coming of dawn,
in our minds, Puck proceeds to 'overcast the night'. His ritual, accom-
panied by magicianly gestures of fog-raising, has the repetitions proper
to incantation, and his own explicit phrase makes him for the moment
a sinister, formidable figure:

> **Up and down, up and down,**
> **I will lead them up and down:**
> **I am fear'd in field and town.**
> **Goblin, lead them up and down.**

But his will o'the wisp manipulation of the quartet of lovers is more
engagingly mischievous than sinister. Distorting his higher pitch to
imitate the men's voices, he preserves the metre and the rhyme-scheme
of his mortal dupes, and leads them astray in the intenser darkness which
is created in the daylit theatre by the words and miming of the actors.
Doors and Study-space are brought into play, and the Stage-Posts
too, as the actors dodge round them, to convey the sense of a labyrinth
in the darkness. The stage-directions of the Folio, although incom-
plete, are guides to the actors, closely related to the dialogue, and bring
us nearer to the atmosphere of performance in the playhouse: *shifting*

places . . . lye down . . . Sleepe. But although they are fallen in **dark uneven way,** and although the night remains **weary** and **long** and **tedious,** as the lovers in turn give up the chase and decide to take some sleep, each contributes to the sense of approaching daylight by looking towards the angle of Aurora's harbinger: the impression is strengthened in their words: **Come thou gentle day . . . thy grey light . . . if ever I thy face by day-light see . . . By day's approach look to be visited.** Helena continues the process (glancing in the same direction) in her prayer, **shine comforts from the East.** She is allowed just one compact stanza of six lines, the shape much loved by Shakespeare as we have already seen (A B A B C C):* in this short space she enlarges upon her misery and composes herself to sleep. There is a special and characteristic charm in her last line when, after speaking of how the others **detest** her **company,** she begs sleep to

> **Steal me awhile from mine own company.**

With three of his victims laid to rest, Puck then quickens the pulse to tetrameters, a measure more suitable to his delight in his successful machinations:

> **Yet but three? Come one more,**
> **Two of both kinds makes up four.**
> **Here she comes,**

(what did I tell you?)

> **curst and sad.**
> **Cupid is a knavish lad,**
> **Thus to make poor females mad.**

He recognises Cupid as a kindred spirit. It is appropriate that Hermia's stanza should repeat Helena's pattern: confusion is being reduced to order, both in the formal pattern in which they are led to their places on the Stage and in the varying but equally formal pattern of their speech and Puck's. The misery of Hermia's discomfiture is vividly

* See *page* 87, *above.*

realised in her words: she is **bedabbled with the dew, and torn with briars**, she **can no further crawl**. Poor little vixen! But she still holds our affection, for in spite of everything, her goodnight prayer, as she too awaits **the break of day**, is

Heavens shield Lysander, if they mean a fray.

It remains for Robin to compose the quarrel he has provoked. This is simply done, by applying the antidote to the sleeping Lysander's eye. He has already disposed of the lovers in their destined pairs, and now he speaks over them a general lullaby, with yet another metrical effect, shortening his rhymes to dimeters, and rounding the second pair with a third, and longer, rhyming line:

> **On the ground**
> **Sleep sound:**
> **I'll apply**
> **To your eye,**
> **Gentle lover, remedy.**

Such seems to be the arrangement concealed under the compressed lineation of both Quarto and Folio. Still casting his spell, he repeats the stanza-pattern a second time. Then for explanation he reverts to tetrameters:

> **And the Country Proverb known,**
> **That every man should take his own,**
> **In your waking shall be shown.**

The final comment runs off at a gallop, which expresses in sound the essence of Puck's humour and the gay unravelling of this comedy of errors:

> **Jack shall have Jill,**
> **Naught shall go ill,**
> **The man shall have his Mare again, and all shall be well.**

Thereupon he disappears. The agile Tooley has, in fact, jumped down into the Trap-Door.

*   *   *

[IV.i] *They sleepe all the Act* is the stage-direction of the Folio. Since the word 'Act', although it could mean a sequence of action on the stage (the usual modern sense), often signified a pause in performance, it is possible that at some period of the play's acting-history before 1623 there was an interval at this point—perhaps others earlier in the play, for at the private theatres, the Blackfriars for instance, the candles had to be attended to periodically; and this was probably true of any private performance of this play.[16] A special problem is presented by the presence of the sleeping lovers, who cannot of course walk off stage, and were evidently not to be accommodated behind the curtain-line of the Study. They were, therefore, it seems (in private performance) left 'sleeping' in view of the audience during the intermission. In the public theatre there were no candles, but the lovers must, in any event, be so exposed to view for the first 130-odd lines of the ensuing action, during which time the Stage is twice filled with a numerous company—first by the Fairies, then by the Duke's hunt. Clearly the sleepers must not be so placed as to impede the action on the Stage itself, but two pairs of recumbent figures, with a distinguishing distance between them, could hardly be disposed entirely within the Study area; besides, as we shall see, the Study is bespoke. Therefore the lovers must be placed as near as is convenient to the front of the Stage, lying perhaps in their pairs well outside each Stage-Post. The problem and its solution bring us unusually near to morning debates between author and book-keeper.

[1-51] Meanwhile bed-room must be found for Bottom too: *Enter Queene of Fairies, and Clowne, and Fairies, and the King behinde them.* Bottom is led (the Ass-head as good as blindfolding the actor) by the Queen's Fairies, and she invites him to sit down **upon this flow'ry bed.** It is a phrase we have heard before: it was not long ago that an angel woke her from her 'flow'ry bed'. Now she will rest upon this same bed (the moss-bank in the Study which Oberon once decked in speech with wild thyme, musk-roses and eglantine), and her angel will lower his bulk to the rush-strewn ground at her feet. Her pleasure, as she sits among the flowers, is to crown him with **musk roses** and to kiss the **fair large ears** of the property-head. *The King behinde them* watches the incongruous picture with satisfaction. A discrepancy in the printed texts confronts us here. Bottom, employing the services of his fairy attendants, bids Peaseblossom **Scratch my head**. A little later he tells Mustardseed **to help Cavalery Cobweb to scratch**. Meanwhile he has dispatched Cobweb on a soldier's errand to **get your weapons in your hand, and kill me a red-hipp'd humble-Bee, on the top of a thistle**. If Peaseblossom, with his military helmet in the shape of a pea-flower, was formerly the sentinel (beside Titania's couch) shanghaied at Oberon's command, the task of killing the bee for his **honey-bag** seems properly his. Bottom, recalling his previous interruptions of Quince ('To the rest, yet my chief humour is for a tyrant . . . Now name the rest of the Players. This is Ercles' vein . . .'), stops the **good Mounsieur** two or three times as he tries to set off on his errand, with a mortal's ponderous humour about his diminutive size. Little Mustardseed (the name expresses his especially minute stature) is naturally reluctant to give his hand to the hairy monster—**Give me your neaf, Mounsieur Mustardseed**—and expresses his diffidence in an excess of **courtesy**, an unending succession of timid bows. Titania invites her **sweet love** to **hear some music**. Instead of the delicate harmonies of fairy song, he opts for **the tongs and the bones**, and the Folio text informs us that the back-stage men provided on this cue *Musicke Tongs, Rurall Musicke*. The cacophony is abruptly but tactfully curtailed by the Queen's next question (as always, by contrast to Bottom's prose, her utterances do their best to preserve the dignity of verse): **Or say sweet Love, what thou desirest to eat**. In his character of Ass, Bottom chooses **your good dry Oats . . . good hay, sweet hay** (the words suggest the braying of the donkey) **hath no fellow**. But then **an exposition of sleep** (he means 'disposition': Kemp and his fellows anticipated Mrs Malaprop) comes upon him. And (all the fairies dismissed, vanishing **all ways away**, by the Doors, into the Study, down through the Trap-Door) we are left with the monumental picture of the Fairy Queen with the Ass-head in her lap: the situation has its poetical comment from the

Queen herself, using the imagery appropriate to her cradle, 'Quite over-canopi'd with luscious woodbine':

> **So doth the woodbine the sweet Honeysuckle**
> **Gently entwist; the female Ivy so**
> **Enrings the barky fingers of the Elm.**
> **O how I love thee! how I dote on thee!**

[52-108] Her dotage is thus explicitly dramatised, in posture and in speech, and it excites the pity of her lord as he comes forward from his retirement, and points out to Puck, newly arrived at his elbow, **this sweet sight**. He tells him then (and us) of a meeting, which we have not seen, **behind the wood**. The speech is informative exposition, but it is more than mere narration; it expresses his distaste for her shame, and makes use of a remarkable conceit to suggest the appropriate attitude of outraged propriety: Titania, he tells us, **had rounded** the **hairy temples** of the Ass

> **With coronet of fresh and fragrant flowers.**
> **And that same dew which sometime on the buds,**
> **Was wont to swell like round and orient pearls,**
> **Stood now within the pretty flouriets' eyes,**
> **Like tears that did their own disgrace bewail.**

Affected by this mood, the Queen became mild and pliable and gave up **her changeling child**, the cause of all their dispute.

> **And now I have the Boy, I will undo**
> **This hateful imperfection of her eyes.**

The phrase expresses vividly the offence to Fairy dignity which has come from the Queen's humiliation. Puck is now commanded to

> **take this transformed scalp,**
> **From off the head of this Athenian swain**

—and the King again suggests the visionary quality of the main action of this play: Bottom and **the other** sleeping mortals, to whom our attention is once more drawn, are to

> **... think no more of this night's accidents,**
> **But as the fierce vexation of a dream.**

The recurring note inevitably reminds the audience of the play's advertised title, and it will be struck again and again in the last phases of the story. We see now why all the sleepers should remain on the Stage: as he speaks of the ending of the dream and the resumption of every-day life, he is surrounded by his six anaesthetised patients, and the night of accidents is delicately brought to a close.

As the King, using the familiar incantatory metre, applies the antidote to the Queen's eyes, Puck draws the Ass-head away from her lap, ready to remove the scalp. The complicated movement of the following passage is swiftly and skilfully written in to the text of the dialogue: we have the stages of Titania's waking and realisation:

> **Methought I was enamoured of an Ass.**
> **—There lies your love.**
> **—How came these things to pass?**
> **Oh, how mine eyes do loathe his visage now!**

The outcry of disgust is left rhymeless by the King's soothing interruption:

> **Silence awhile. Robin, take off this head ...**

The demand for music to

> **strike more dead**
> **Than common sleep of all these five the sense ...**

leads again to an interruption of the series of couplet-rhymes, by the Queen's obedient call:

Music, ho music, such as charmeth sleep.

And Puck, at the moment of decapitation, slily slips in his private rhyme:

Now, when thou wak'st, with thine own fool's eyes peep.

One can but marvel at the dramatic virtuosity of Shakespeare's versification, preserved to us through all the sometimes unreliable transmission of the early printed texts. The stately dance of the King and Queen has its dramatic purpose too. With lullaby-music sounding from the Tiring-House, they

. . . rock the ground whereon these sleepers be.

They visit each of the five with ritual gestures of hypnosis, and Oberon seals their reconciliation with six lines which hauntingly repeat the rhyme of the couplet with which he introduced the dance; and as he speaks, he reminds us of the once-expected, long-forgotten dénouement to which the whole play is leading. At their first angry encounter, Titania had spoken scornfully of the 'bouncing Amazon' who 'to Theseus must be Wedded' and taunted her lord with having come to Athens 'to give their bed joy and prosperity'. Now the King and Queen, **new in amity,**

. . . will tomorrow midnight, solemnly
Dance in Duke Theseus' house triumphantly,
And bless it to all fair prosperity.

It is an occasion we may anticipate with eager curiosity, but (such is the playwright's cunning) we shall have forgotten it again before it comes. It is once more Puck's task to break in upon this peaceful cadence: the change of metre reflects the change of mood:

Fairy King attend, and mark,
I do hear the morning Lark.

A moment or two before this, his ear has been cocked in the direction of 'Aurora's harbinger'. It is noticeable that Oberon and Titania adopt Puck's tetrameters but translate his fidgety alarm into their own mood of wistful dignity: the King's former boast of making sport 'with the morning's love' seems forgotten now, as they circle the perimeter of the Stage and depart: their flight has a haunting beauty:

> **Then my Queen, in silence sad,**
> **Trip we after night's shade;**
> **We the Globe can compass soon,**
> **Swifter than the wand'ring Moon.**

It is our last sight of the moon, as the King and Queen gaze up at the inevitable quarter of the playhouse roof. Puck, the Ass-head in his hands, is left momentarily alone. *Sleepers Lye still*, says the Folio, reminding us (by this imperative instruction to the actors) of their continued presence, the four lovers at the front of the Stage, Bottom sleeping off his nightmare on the moss-bank.[17] From the Tiring-House behind one of the Doors, a sudden sound startles Puck out of his wits. *Winde Hornes*, bids the Folio. It is the most recognisable, the most evocative of all musical sounds, the note of the hunting-horn. It is moreover a master-stroke of theatrical effect on the playwright's part.

[109-192] For we must remember that, having created and sustained the illusion of moon-lit darkness in his daylit playhouse, he now has the problem of dispelling that illusion. What better embodiment of the coming of daylight could be desired than the music of the horns, the barking of the hounds (expertly mimicked in the Tiring-House), and the visible paraphernalia (bows and spears and cloaks and boots) of the hunt itself? No wonder Puck darts to ground (through the Trap-Door) at the first note of the horn. The brilliant coloured clothes of the hunting-party will already do much to dispel the atmosphere created by the vegetable earth-colours of the Fairies' dresses and the subfusc of the eloping lovers. It seems possible that the Chamberlain's Men included a picnic-breakfast in the bustle of this moment, with pages spreading a carpet at Hippolyta's feet, and offering her chicken-bones and stirrup-cups from a hamper. The model for such a

scene can be found in the picture of an Assembly, made in the presence
of Queen Elizabeth, from Turberville's *The Noble Art of Venerie*, 1575
(the picture is conveniently accessible in *Shakespeare's England*, vol. II,
345). We may also admire at this point another skilful stroke in Shakespeare's dramaturgy. His plot requires here that the Duke should discover
the lovers asleep in the wood. How then is the Duke to be induced to
come to the wood at crack of dawn? The solution, as simple as it seems
inevitable, is to bring him out hunting. And there is no more suitable
diversion for the entertainment of Hippolyta, the Amazon, during the
tedious gap of four days before their 'nuptial hour'.[18]

But, as always, Shakespeare's chief weapon is the spoken word: and
this is the explanation of the expansively discursive twenty-five lines
that follow. We have already been skilfully and economically prepared for the coming of day. Now the poet is projecting in poetical
terms, for his necessary theatrical effect, the hunt, the landscape and
the early morning. The bushes and the brakes, the briars and thorns
of the night are displaced by **the Western valley** and **the Mountain's
top.** We are carried, by **the vaward of the day** and the picture of
the drooping ears of the Duke's hounds **that sweep away the morning dew,** far from the bank 'quite over-canopi'd with luscious woodbine, With sweet musk roses, and with Eglantine' where 'sleeps
Titania, sometime of the night, Lull'd in these flowers, with dances
and delight'. Oberon himself has anticipated the imagery of morning:
we have heard that he walks abroad in the dawn 'like a Forester':
now Theseus sends to **find out the Forester.** And the rival praises of
the voices of those Spartan hounds—Hippolyta's with **gallant chiding . . . So musical a discord, such sweet thunder,** and Theseus's
match'd in mouth like bells . . .

> **A cry more tunable**
> **Was never halloo'd to, nor cheer'd with horn,**
> **In Crete, in Sparta, nor in Thessaly**

—all these phrases give descriptive substance and the added power of
associative overtones from legend and literature to the enthusiastic
mimicry which will be provided by the back-stage men in the Tiring-

House. **Judge when you hear**, says the Duke. Yet for a moment, he checks his order for the hounds to give tongue:

> **But soft, what nymphs are these?**

Egeus, with his sharp nose, has ferreted out the sleeping quartet and expresses his wonder **of their being here together**. The Duke graciously offers a probable explanation:

> **No doubt they rose up early, to observe**
> **The rite of May . . .**

This line has caused some trouble to those critics who have tried to relate the play precisely to the calendar (does the action take place on the eve of May-day or at the Midsummer of the title?). Such speculation is almost as little relevant to Shakespeare's dramatic purpose as the attempt to calculate the play's duration and the phases of its moon. At this moment the poet wishes to bring into play all the associations of May-day ritual, of festivity, of the reviving year. These same associations of May-day 'observance' were called up at the moment when the lovers first planned their flight to the forest (I.i.167). Theseus too seems now to have performed an **observation** of this kind. The wholesale transference of the Athenian gentry into the woods seems to bear some of the festival quality of the May-day ceremony.[19] In the context of the narrative, however, the precise date in the year is less important than the fact, suddenly remembered by Theseus, that this is **the day That Hermia should give answer of her choice**. As he bids the huntsmen wake them with their horns, we are reminded momentarily of his stern and formidable judgement in the opening scene of the play. But our apprehension hardly survives the cheerful sound of the horns and the hallooing off-stage (*Hornes and they wake. Shout within, they all start up*) and the Duke's good-humoured raillery:

> **Good morrow friends: Saint Valentine is past.**
> **Begin these woodbirds but to couple now?**

Those who wake from sleep and find themselves in the midst of an inquisitive and smiling company are fair game for mockery: and the bewildered and embarrassed faces of the startled four provoke the laughter not only of the hunting-party but of the whole playhouse. Lysander, of course, is still under the influence of Puck's antidote, and his halting words, **half sleep, half waking**, do not find coherent sense or syntax until, his waking eye focusing upon Hermia, he remembers:

> **I came with Hermia hither. Our intent**
> **Was to be gone from Athens, where we might**
> **Without the peril of the Athenian Law . . .**

He is not allowed to finish his sentence. The testy Egeus, barking his iterations with the explosive style of which John Heminges was clearly the master (and Shakespeare's inspiration), invokes again the cruel justice of the earlier scene:

> **Enough, enough, my Lord: you have enough;**
> **I beg the Law, the Law upon his head:**
> **They would have stol'n away, they would, Demetrius . . .**

Among the many resemblances between this play and ROMEO AND JULIET (which may have immediately preceded it) is the verbal style Shakespeare developed for Capulet and Egeus; he could trust Heminges to make the most of it. Demetrius, however, no longer supports his would-be father-in-law: his explanation to the Duke is more coherent than Lysander's, but he too is at a loss to account for his change of heart—

> **I wot not by what power,**
> **(But by some power it is) . . .**

Nevertheless he is wholesomely convinced that he has once more come to his **natural taste**. Theseus is quick to size up the situation, though not at once its causes: **Of this discourse we more will hear anon.** However, he does not hestiate in his decision to **over-bear** the

destiny

like the Tempest they all move towards a point — all is resolved.

110

will of Egeus, for, as Chaucer said of his Theseus, as he pardoned the rival lovers in the wood, 'pitee renneth soone in gentil herte': he proposes a triple wedding, and (with a glance in the direction of Aurora's harbinger, **for the morning now is something worn**) sets aside **our purpos'd hunting**. It may be guessed that this last decision is not agreeable to his Amazon lady, and the Duke's **Come Hippolyta** includes in its inflection a hint of 'Come, come, no sulking: we can go hunting any day of the week'. The horn and the barking of the hounds accompany their departure, and are heard fading into the distance.

[193-205] The Duke has determined to hear more anon of the lovers' discourse: when next we see him, he and Hippolyta will be discussing what the lovers have told them. Meanwhile we have, by way of *coda*, a charming glimpse of the lovers' state of mind. Each in turn expresses bewilderment and uncertainty: only Lysander, still affected by Puck's drug, is silent. The tentative search for reality finds its fullest expression in Demetrius's question:

> **Are you sure**
> **That we are awake? It seems to me,**
> **That yet we sleep, we dream.**

Gradually, as the play advances to its close, the 'Dream' of the title is insinuated as a motif into our minds. The pace quickens as bewilderment gives way to realisation:

> **Do not you think**
> **The Duke was here, and bid us follow him?**
> **—Yea, and my Father.**
> **—And Hippolyta.**
> **—And he did bid us follow to the Temple.**

And so they trip off two by two, following the Duke, and their diversion **by the way** will be to **recount** their **dreams**.

[206-226] The audience will be wondering what is to happen next; the groundlings stretching their legs, as their habit is when a

scene is over, and ready to gossip till the next entry cuts short their chat. But then Kemp's well-known voice, heard from his pillow on that flowery bed in the Study, reminds them that the Stage is after all not empty, and the prospect of a comic turn from their favourite clown is not unwelcome. But Shakespeare has no mind to give Will Kemp his head: he knows him too well for that. Bottom's awakening is entirely in character, and entirely within the context of the play: **When my cue comes, call me, and I will answer.** He imagines himself still at rehearsal, still at the precise moment when at Quince's bidding he entered 'into that Brake' (III.i.92). But a prodigious yawn (**Hey ho**) shakes some of the sleep from his eyes, and he looks round for his companions. With growing awareness, a scaled crescendo of intensity and volume in calling their names ends in a mighty bellow for the deaf **Starveling?** (no better name for a cry that echoes through the empty wood). **God's my life! Stolen hence, and left me asleep?** Kemp's expression of indignant astonishment melts into a slow-spreading smile of ecstatic reminiscence: **I have had a most rare vision. I have had a dream, past the wit of man, to say; what dream it was.** The punctuation of the Fisher Quarto, reflected almost exactly in the Folio, is eloquent of Kemp's (and Shakespeare's) timing in the delivery of this speech. **Man is but an Ass,** (the comma represents the abrupt hesitation on the ominous word, and a side-long glance at the rush-strewn floor where he has just been sleeping) **if he go about to expound this dream.** (Again it will be noticed that the motif of the 'dream' gathers weight.) Bottom must reassure himself by feeling with his hands the air in front of his face where the Ass's nose has been: **Methought I was,** (and then with relief) **there is no man can tell what.** He must feel above his head where the long ears were, and might still be: **Methought I was, and methought I had.** And again with relief: **But man is but a patch'd fool, if he will offer to say, what methought I had.** The Pauline travesty (**The eye of man hath not heard . . .**) follows briskly and rhetorically, as a release from anxiety: it is one of Kemp's gimmicks, but it can be made to suit the moment. Then his face lights up with new inspiration: **I will get Peter Quince to write a Ballett of this dream** (will it be 'written in eight and six'? we wonder):[20] and Kemp is allowed to throw one of his corny jokes at the groundlings: **it shall be called 'Bottom's Dream'; because it hath no bottom.** The ballett is to be sung **in the latter end of a play, before the Duke**; and Bottom's aspiring soul soars to a rapture of ambition as he contemplates the ideal moment for the première of 'Bottom's Dream': **Peradventure, to make it the more gracious, I shall sing it at her death.** We do not need to be told that he is thinking of the climax of *the most lamentable Comedy, and most cruel death of Pyramus and Thisbe.* Cheerfully he trudges off by one of the Doors on his way back to Athens, and the Study-curtains are closed for the first time since the scene of Titania's lullaby.

*　　　*　　　*

We shall see no more of the flowery bank and the hawthorn-brake, and it is a fit moment to consider how the conditions of the unlocalised Stage have made possible Shakespeare's evocation of his wood near Athens. His chief instruments have been the miming and posture and gesture of his actors, and above all the words he has given them to speak. It has been a dangerous place, where mortals are at the mercy of wild beasts, where misled night-wanderers are chased in panic 'thorough bog, thorough bush, thorough brake, thorough briar', where thorns snatch at their apparel; there are bears, boars, pards and crawling serpents, and the miniature hazards are black beetles, newts and blindworms, thorny hedgehogs and the clamorous owl. It is moreover uncomfortable; the altering of the seasons has brought mud and rain; the ground is dank and dirty, and makes a cold bed; the lovers are fogbound and bedabbled with the dew and torn with briars. But it is also a place of delight, decked with honeysuckle and musk-roses and the nodding violet; there are primrose beds; there are humble-bees and painted butterflies; the mouth waters at the sound of that diet of apricocks and dewberries, purple grapes, green figs and mulberries; there are squirrels and glow-worms and pretty flowerets and the nightingale. The variety of this atmosphere suggests inconsistency, but the inconsistency is Shakespeare's and it is intentional. At one time he is at pains to emphasise the danger, at another the discomfort; but then again the immediate context needs the mood of dances and delight, of maidenly childhood rambling. It is the uncluttered flexibility of the unlocalised Stage that makes this possible, and the director who would try to stress one aspect in preference to (and to the exclusion of) another, as any method of scenic realism must force him to do, is frustrating Shakespeare's kaleidoscopic purpose.

*   *   *

[IV.ii.1-47] The words of the next scene impose no particular locality upon the players, but we may be sure that Pope and his fellows will make it unmistakably clear to us that we are out of the wood, and back to the every-day life of Athens: if, when the Chamber-curtains open, we find ourselves once more in the confined space of the carpenter's shop, where we first met the mechanicls, the sense of returning home will be strengthened. The contrast to Bottom's good cheer is highly effective. A deep depression hangs over all—even over the printers of the Quarto, who, forgetting that Flute and Thisbe are the same person, tell us: *Enter Quince, Flute, Thisby and the rabble.* Rescuing *Snout* and *Starveling* from this ignominious description, the Folio distributes the speeches with more probability. It is old Starveling who gives the weight of his experience to the opinion about Bottom's fate, that **Out of doubt he is transported.** Flute's words have all the pathos of the young hopeful's first big disappointment in life: **If he come not, then the play is marr'd. It goes not forward, doth it?** His admiration for Bottom's talent is unbounded, and shared (in the subject's absence) even by Quince: **you have not a man in all Athens, able to discharge Pyramus but he.** Snug's news of the triple wedding only aggravates the sense of lost opportunity, and rouses in Flute a sort of keening elegy for **sweet bully Bottom.** What distresses him most is the chance of enrichment that Bottom has missed: there is a special charm in his iterative lament for his colleague's loss of that princely sum: **thus hath he lost sixpence a day, during his life; he could not have scaped sixpence a day. An the Duke had not given him sixpence a day for playing Pyramus, I'll be hang'd. He would have deserved it. Sixpence a day in Pyramus, or nothing.**

Into this quintessence of gloom bursts Bottom, with all the old assurance of his exuberant optimism: **Where are these Lads? Where are these hearts?** He prepares them to hear wonders, then, in face of their gaping curiosity, draws back, with a see-saw of give-and-take which Kemp knows well how to handle: **Masters, I am to discourse wonders; but ask me not what . . . I will tell you every thing right as it fell out . . . Not a word of me.** There is but one thing he will tell them, and with all the comedian's skill he delays the climax of his news: **. . . the Duke hath dined** (that cannot be the news). **Get your apparel together, good strings to your beards, new ribands to your pumps, meet presently at the Palace, every man look o'er his part: for the short and the long is,** (at last, after an expressive comma, it comes) **our play is preferred**—it is on the short list of recommendations. The general jubilation is but momentarily checked by Bottom's teasing advice: Flute is coy about his **clean linen**; Snug is shown how to use his nails **for the Lion's claws**; and while so explaining, Bottom catches wind of the **Garlic** on his breath. It is all good music-hall routine, and Kemp is given his pride of place in the centre of the act. But it is all in character for its context in the narrative, and the audience is promised some uproarious entertainment at the Palace wedding, which we have (right from the start) been prepared to expect as the dénouement of the play. **No more words**, then. **Away, go away.** Quince, the book-keeper, is seen hurriedly gathering up his 'scrip' and the actors' 'parts', as the Chamber-curtains close on the carpenter's shop.

*   *   *

[V.i] We should at this point remember that what we are reconstructing is a performance on one of those 'sundry times' when the play was 'publickely acted, by the Right honourable, the Lord Chamberlaine his servants'. We are concerned with a performance of the finally revised version, the manuscript copy (Shakespeare's 'foul papers') from which Fisher's Quarto was probably printed. We may imagine Shakespeare as reflecting to himself that he had considerably strengthened his play since it was first performed some six or more years earlier. At that time it might seem that the plot of the play had been wound up by the end of Act IV: Oberon is reconciled to Titania,

the lovers have sorted themselves in the right pairs, Bottom's transla-
tion and his 'most rare vision' are over—what more is there to expect?
Nothing but the wedding-ceremonies, and of course the performance
of that 'Interlude' which was designed to take place 'before the Duke
and the Duchess, on his wedding day at night', and the promised
visitation of the Fairies to bless Duke Theseus's house 'to all fair
prosperity'. Sufficient material for a dénouement in the circumstances
of a court-wedding, where ritual elegance and graceful diplomatic
allusion are more important than dramatic vitality. But to send home
contented those keen critics in the twopenny gallery of the public
playhouse, something more is needed, a motif which will knit the
whole scene—if such is possible, the whole play—into a coherent
harmony. The person to impose this harmony is the presiding Duke
and patron and bridegroom. For the public audiences, perhaps, Shakespeare enriched the role of Theseus by presenting him as an enlightened
patron of the arts and a kindly critic of even the incompetent amateur.
By so doing, he was offering the audience a mirror-image of themselves, and making a plea for their sympathetic reception of the
Chamberlain's Men's efforts. As Theseus instructs his court, and even
his newly-wed bride, in a proper generosity of appreciation, he is, by
a favourite device of bluff, hoping that his audience will mistake the
pretence for the reality. His part, in Shakespeare's final version, is
written with much sympathy and humour—and not the least delightful feature of the portrait is that, for all its intelligence and sensibility
and generous wisdom, he is not always right.

[1-28] Meanwhile there is, once again, a technical problem of
transition. When Bottom left the wood to return to Athens, the
Study-curtains were closed, and our attention was immediately caught
and absorbed by activity in the Chamber above. Now that the
Chamber-curtains are closed again, our eyes (and our imagination)
return to the Stage below. This is bare, except that it is covered with
rushes, that there are leafy boughs still attached to the Stage-Posts, and
that (though we have not noticed it for a long time) the central Trap-
Door is open. Above this Trap-Door the Duke's attendants now con-
struct a fire (the Duke's hearth) with fire-dogs, and logs and brush-
wood, and smoke rising from below the Trap. This is a necessary

feature of the scene (derived perhaps from the original conception of performance in 'the great chamber' of some private house) for the kindling of the tapers which the Fairies will carry or wear, like Mistress Page's Windsor 'Urchins, Ouphs, and Fairies, green and white, With rounds of waxen Tapers on their heads'.[21] The fire is twice alluded to in the text: Puck tells us, as the embers sink, that 'Now the wasted brands do glow . . .', and Oberon's command to the Fairies, as they kindle their tapers, begins 'Through the house give glimmering light, By the dead and drowsy fire'. Moreover, if the fire seems an anomaly in summer, we have Titania's authority for the alteration of the seasons (II.i.107 ff.). For the rest, rushes are no less appropriate indoors than out of doors in the Elizabethan period, and the leafy boughs on the Stage-Posts are simply disposed of by the attendants by pitching them into the Trap-Door as fuel for their fire: in their place they hang branched candelabra, which help at once to make us feel indoors at night, and festive. To his own fireside the Duke leads his newly-wed bride, and their philosophy is uttered at leisure, as they gaze reflectively down into the flames or up at the rising smoke.

Their conversation picks up a thread (in Shakespeare's habitual narrative method) from the end of a previous scene: 'Of this discourse', Theseus said to the lovers, 'we more will hear anon' (IV.i.184). Now it is Hippolyta who seems the more impressed by what they have heard:

> 'Tis strange, my Theseus, that these lovers speak of.
> —More strange than true.

Her husband protests himself a constitutional sceptic:

> I never may believe
> These antic fables, nor these Fairy toys.

All a fairy-tale, is his verdict on the lovers' account: and his choice of derisory epithet has an irony which we share with the poet at his expense. Then he lectures his bride (and us) on the deluding power of the imagination:[22] **Lovers and mad men** are the exemplary victims of such delusion—and then he adds, with the significantly delayed emphasis of an afterthought, a third category: **and the Poet. . . .** Tongue deep in cheek, and gazing into the flames at his feet (into the Trap-Door of 'Hell'), he quizzes the lunatic:

> **One sees more devils than vast hell can hold;**
> **That is the mad man.**

Next he laughs at the **Lover**, who

> **all as frantic,**
> **Sees Helen's beauty in a brow of Egypt.**

(Hermia, poor 'Ethiope' and 'tawny Tartar', has a brow of Egypt.) But then he turns his raillery upon **the Poet's eye**, and in illustrative caricature, shows it to us **in a fine frenzy rolling**, shows us how it **doth glance from heaven to earth, from earth to heaven**, shows us again how

> **. . . as imagination bodies forth**
> **The forms of things unknown, the Poet's pen**

(he poises the quill above the paper)

> **Turns them to shapes, and gives to airy nothing,**
> **A local habitation, and a name.**

For all the mockery, it is a vivid and accurate portrait, Shakespeare's self-portrait. The 'glorious quip', Dover Wilson calls it, and he speaks of the 'mood of confident self-banter' which 'produced the jest at the expense of "the poet" ' (*New Cambridge* edition, 86, 140). But in its dramatic context, it is something more than this: for the intelligent Theseus, the apostle of **cool reason**, is mocking at his own creator; and yet, after all, throughout the afternoon in the playhouse we have experienced the creative power of the poet's pen; Theseus himself is among his creations, and it may be that before the afternoon is out, the mockery of this sceptical Duke, who cannot believe in 'Fairy toys', will recoil, however gently, upon himself. Meanwhile he shows no trace of his own vulnerability: he is entirely confident in his diagnosis of what we now call wishful thinking:

> **Such tricks hath strong imagination,**
> **That if it would but apprehend some joy,**
> **It comprehends some bringer of that joy.**

Solemn editors have rejected the last two lines of this famous speech,[23] but they are entirely in keeping with the quizzical mood of the speaker, they reflect the general tenour of the strange tales 'that these lovers speak of', and they invoke once again the imagery of the wood in which so much of the action of the play has taken place:

> **Or in the night, imagining some fear,**
> **How easy is a bush suppos'd a Bear!**

Hippolyta, the Amazon, is shrewder than her lord: with downright horse-sense she points out that **all the story of the night**, as told by the lovers, hangs together: it isn't merely imagination, it is more than **fancy's images,**

> **And grows to something of great constancy.**

Moreover she has the modesty to admit that she cannot explain it: it is **strange, and admirable.** As she harps a second time upon her first judgement—' 'Tis strange'—a little touch of obstinacy is written into her role. And there for the moment the debate rests, for (pat upon their cue, like the catastrophe of the old comedy)—

> **Here come the lovers, full of joy and mirth.**

[29-84] After an exchange of salutations, the Duke calls for some entertainment,

To wear away this long age of three hours,
Between our after supper, and bed-time . . .

The appropriate person to organise such entertainment is **our usual manager of mirth**, Philostrate, whom we have seen at the opening of the play: as on that occasion, he is once again given the task of abridging the tedious interval of waiting, the commission to awake the 'nimble spirit of mirth'. He represents a familiar and influential figure at the Elizabethan court, whose office was of crucial importance in affecting the interests of the Chamberlain's Men, the Master of the Revels: it was this functionary who chose the plays to be acted at court, and read manuscripts and attended rehearsals for this purpose. He too therefore—like the ducal patron, the courtly audience, the players and their book-keeper—is a part of that mirror-image of the life and fortunes and aspirations of Shakespeare's company. It is not unlikely that Philostrate showed some touches of topical caricature. There is a discrepancy of speech-headings at this point between Quarto and Folio. The Quarto presents, as we expect, Philostrate answering the Duke's summons: the Folio, substituting Egeus for Philostrate in the stage-direction at the head of the scene, has Theseus calling Egeus (an improbable choice) as 'our usual manager of mirth'. This variation clearly reflects a performance of a later date, in which it was found convenient for an accomplished speaker in the role of Egeus (was it Mr. Editor Heminges?) to take over the manager's speeches in Act V, while the part of Philostrate was relegated to a brief and speechless appearance at the start of Act I. We might simply ignore the incongruous makeshift of the Folio, and follow the Quarto's ascription. But a further difference may suggest a minor readjustment in practice. **There is a brief**, says the 'manager of mirth', **how many sports are ripe.** In the Quarto text, Theseus both reads out the items of the 'brief' and comments on them: in the Folio Lysander (not Egeus) reads the items and the Duke makes his comments in alternating couplets. Perhaps, in the performance reported by the Folio, the reading of the brief was thought one degree too far in incongruity from the previously established character of Egeus. But the fact that the speech was so divided hints at an earlier practice (not implied in the Quarto) which fits the situation much better than the undivided monologue of the Duke. We suggest that Philostrate, the Master of the Revels, presents the bill of fare for approval and selection: **Make choice of which your Highness will see first**. He reads the items and the Duke comments.

If this is the correct disposition, then it becomes clear that Philostrate's presentation of his programme is, on its own small scale, a comic turn for a skilled character-actor. The flourishes of his announcement, delivered with a self-indulgent bravura of elocution, are increasingly tiresome to the Duke, who drily rejects each offering in turn (**We'll none of that . . . That is an old device . . .**): they are indeed old-fashioned, the commonplace clichés of the masque-market. But Philostrate's third suggestion, spoken in a lugubrious tone of mock-elegy—

> **The thrice three Muses, mourning for the death**
> **Of learning, late deceas'd in beggary**

—conceals a topical allusion, readily intelligible to Shakespeare's first audiences, but remaining an enigma today. It evokes from Theseus a different tone: **Satire keen and critical** has its place in the personal polemics of the Elizabethan literary world, but it does not sort well with **a nuptial ceremony** or with the more gracious world of this play. Then comes the item we have been expecting, and it is no accident that Quince's prospectus is, unlike the others, unmetrical:

> **A tedious brief Scene of young Pyramus,**
> **And his love Thisbe; very tragical mirth.**

Immediately the Duke's interest is aroused by the contradictions in the terms of the manifesto: as he asks for enlightenment, he pokes sophisticated fun at the paradoxes:

> **Merry and tragical? Tedious, and brief?**
> **That is, hot ice, and wondrous strange snow.**
> **How shall we find the concord of this discord?**

Philostrate's answer carries the joke farther, a little too far it seems for the humane Duke; it is patronisingly facetious—the heavy-handed jesting of the third-rate intelligence at those even less well endowed than himself. He labours the four elements of the 'discord' at intolerable length (**as brief, as I have known a play . . . Which makes it tedious . . . And tragical, my noble Lord, it is . . . more merry tears . . .**), and the clipped brevity of the Duke's interrupting question,

What are they that do play it?

should warn him (but does not) that his contemptuous loquacity is out of season. His description of the

Hard-handed men, that work in Athens here,
Which never labour'd in their minds till now . . .

is an apt enough account of Quince and his company; and to Philostrate this means that the play is unsuitable for the Duke's entertainment. It is the contempt implicit in Philostrate's manner which causes a significant change of tone in the Duke's response. The mockery vanishes and is replaced by a simple decision:

And we will hear it.

When Philostrate misunderstands Theseus, assuming that he looks to

find sport in their intents,
Extremely stretch'd, and conn'd with cruel pain,

the Duke reiterates his decision:

I will hear that play.

Moreover he supports it with a new and welcome enlightenment of sympathy:

For never any thing can be amiss,
When simpleness and duty tender it.[24]

[85-107] The necessary interval while Philostrate has gone to 'bring them in' is filled with a most interesting exchange between the Duke and Hippolyta. With her typically unimaginative common-sense, she expresses her kind-hearted reluctance

... to see wretchedness o'ercharged;
And duty in his service perishing.

Most graciously and tactfully he embarks on the education of his newly-wed wife:

Why gentle sweet, you shall see no such thing.

And when she quotes at him the opinion of the Master of the Revels,

He says, they can do nothing in this kind ...

his riposte takes the form of an elegant chiasmus, with the added decoration of word-play:

The kinder we, to give them thanks for nothing.

He goes on to describe, in satirical but kindly vein, a scene familiar to some at least of the audience from the royal progresses or state visits to the universities, when

great Clerks have purposed
To greet me with premeditated welcomes.

There is no need to search here (as some sleuth-editors will do) for an allusion to some particular occasion. The lines project, rather, a typical situation of contemporary life, the stage-fright of a commoner unused to the presence of the visiting royalty: and its dramatic importance here is to cast anticipatory light upon the coming appearance of Quince as Prologue, and to guide the reaction of Hippolyta and the courtiers and us in the audience to his pathetic efforts:

> ... I have seen them shiver and look pale,
> Make periods in the midst of sentences,
> Throttle their practis'd accent in their fears,
> And in conclusion, dumbly have broke off,
> Not paying me a welcome.

This passage may be another part of the material added in the play's later revision. It is certainly a cardinal example of that enlightened attitude in the ducal patron which gives a unifying harmony to the whole of Act V. His judgement on the 'great Clerks' invites close attention:

> Trust me sweet,
> Out of this silence yet I pick'd a welcome:
> And in the modesty of fearful duty,
> I read as much, as from the rattling tongue
> Of saucy and audacious eloquence.

The phrase seems a reflection upon Philostrate's loquacity.

> Love therefore, and tongue-tied simplicity,
> In least, speak most, to my capacity.

Throughout the uproarious absurdity of what follows, we shall be aware of the presence, and respectful of the opinion, of this most wise and generous of critics. But meanwhile **the Prologue is address'd**: the ladies have taken their places; and the whole court, attendants and all, settle down to be entertained. They sit in a ring round the perimeter of the Stage, with their backs to us, warming their toes at the fire, and by their close proximity to the audience making us feel the warmth of the blazing logs, as we sit (or stand) round the hearth watching the lamentable comedy through the haze of wood-smoke.

[108-127] Into the midst of this distinguished company, heralded (the Folio tells us) by a flourish of trumpets, through the still-closed

curtains of the Study, blinking in the unexpected glare of the candle-light, his 'scrip' clenched in his hand, comes our old friend Peter Quince—the character already so firmly sketched for us by Thomas Pope. He is in good heart, and why not? He has written his prologue (in ten and ten, as it happens; with a neat scheme of alternate rhymes and a final couplet—sonnet-wise, but with four lines missing) and he embarks upon its delivery with assurance:

If we offend, it is with our good will.

But he cannot proceed with the complicated (but impeccable) compliment of his long opening sentence, because somebody bursts out laughing, and then everybody laughs, because what he has said so far is (in isolation) absurd; and when he is allowed to continue, the rest of the sentence (without its beginning) is equally ridiculous:

That you should think, we come not to offend,
But with good will.

Shakespeare was always adept at composing sentences which could have more than one meaning: and the ambiguity here is not in poor Quince's favour. He never recovers from this bad start. His nerve has gone, and thereafter he proceeds to 'make periods in the midst of sentences'. Some of the consequent confusion is due perhaps to a hasty reference to his 'scrip', which is upside down. A panic acceleration is responsible for the coupling of **All for your delight, We are not here.** At last he realises that his prologue has not gone as he intended, and with an embarrassed courtesy he returns through the curtains to muster his team. Theseus (when Quince is no longer there to hear his judgement) underlines for us the nature of his failure: **This fellow doth not stand upon points.** The punctuation of the Quarto should be closely observed. Dover Wilson reproduces it exactly, 'including the final comma which delightfully suggests the rising tone on which the stage-frighted Quince concludes'. He adds the dry comment that 'it is the only speech in the canon the punctuation of which edd. have hitherto treated with respect'. Incidentally, any Shakespearian actor since Shakespeare's day might take to heart Lysander's **good moral . . . It**

is not enough to speak, but to speak true. The Duke himself perceives that Quince's prologue, if read on paper, is capable of coherent construing: **His speech was like a tangled chain: nothing impaired, but all disordered.** Those members of the audience who are sensitive to the changing rhythms of Shakespeare's dialogue will have perceived that during the performance of 'Pyramus and Thisbe', when our attention is directed to the fustian verse of the mechanicals, by contrast the gentry speak (for the only time in the play) in prose.

[127-156] Who is next? The Folio once again preserves for us the very atmosphere of the playhouse, by recording at this point the instruction: *Tawyer with a Trumpet before them.* Tawyer, as we know, was a playhouse servant, 'Mr. Heminges man'. The curtains of the Study-space are flung open, making more room in the area beyond the fireplace for the manoeuvring of the players. All five of them, preceded by Tawyer's trumpet, enter for the Dumb Show, while Quince expounds their miming to the audience. The Dumb Show, like the later example in HAMLET, is a telegraphic preview of the action of the play. Undeterred by his first failure, Pope's Quince introduces his cast with an engaging assurance. We recognise each in turn under his disguise. It has long been customary for Bottom to play the part of Pyramus with helmet, breastplate and sword: perhaps the tradition is a relic of the 'realistic' performances in which all the characters of the play, from the Duke downwards, wore the costume of a conventional Athenian antiquity, and in which Bottom's dress would appear as a grotesque parody of Theseus's own. It is possible that in Shakespeare's playhouse the mechanicals would have been made to assume some crudely emblematic paraphernalia to suggest the classical past; but there is no reason why Pyramus should be presented as a military man; he is a lover ('more condoling'), not a tyrant, and Peter Quince's introduction of him as a **sweet youth and tall** suggests, rather, a familiar miniature by Nicholas Hilliard: Pyramus should be a mockery, not of Theseus, but of Romeo, or at least Demetrius. His sword, it is true, is a necessary property, but it is as suitable to the amorous Elizabethan gallant as to the classical warrior. Whatever his costume, nothing can conceal the impatient ambition of Bottom (raring to go). Unmistakable too, even if he has chosen to 'play it in a Mask', is the lanky, teenage Flute beneath the flowing gown of **this beauteous Lady, Thisbe**. Snout, following Bottom's prescription at the rehearsal in the wood, has some **lime and rough-cast** about him 'to signify wall'; and we see him 'hold his fingers thus' for the **wall's chink**, while Bottom and Flute go through the motions of whispering, and hurriedly depart in opposite directions, to make way for the introduction of old Starveling, with **Lanthorn, dog, and bush of thorn**: with the abstracted air of deafness and age, he **presenteth moon-shine** to the life, and his companion dog is as real, no doubt, as Launce's dog Crab, who has brought the house down on a previous occasion, imperturbably nonchalant as 'the sourest natured dog that lives', who, in the midst of the family's lamentations at Launce's parting, 'all this while sheds not a tear: nor speaks a word' (Two GENTLEMEN OF VERONA, II.iii.6 ff.). We notice in passing Quince's emphatically correct articulation of **Ninus' tomb**: thither Thisbe returns from the background, to be confronted by **this grisly beast (which Lion hight by name)**. As Snug, in his lion's mask, scares Thisbe away—**or rather did affright**—Quince's anxious eye is turned upon the ladies in case they should 'be afear'd of the Lion': he is relieved—or is he puzzled?—to read nothing in their countenance but amused curiosity. Thisbe's **Mantle** is dropped and mauled, and the Stage once more cleared for the moment of climax: **Anon comes Pyramus**. Bottom's re-entry reminds us of a similar appearance at rehearsal (the début of the 'Ass's nole') and of a vivid parody in Puck's subsequent narration: 'And forth my Mimic comes'. Quince's commentary aspires throughout to eloquence—diffusely larded by Shakespeare with bathos and expletive (in Alexander Pope's sense) and tautology—but it reaches the height of dramatic grandeur in the crisis of Pyramus's alliterative suicide:

**Whereat, with blade, with bloody blameful blade,
He bravely broach'd his boiling bloody breast.**

Bottom must work fast in mime to keep pace with the movement of the story: he will have the opportunity later to spread himself in the leisurely self-indulgence of his death-scene. Flute too makes short work of Thisbe's demise, and Quince concludes the Dumb Show with the traditional finality of a rhymed couplet. Then while the actors prepare for the fray, he plants himself at the corner of the fireplace, holding the 'scrip' as book-keeper of the company—silently mouthing the lines, occasionally prompting, making sure of entries and properties, watching anxiously the audience's reactions, interested but rather puzzled by the courtiers' comments. It is a fruitful opportunity for the comic talents of that excellent actor Thomas Pope, whose sense of character will not permit of irrelevant business which might distract from some necessary question of his play.

The Duke's comments are more indulgent, more helpful to the players, than those of the rest of the court: although he is occasionally betrayed into mockery, he follows his own precept: 'Our sport shall be, to take what they mistake; And what poor duty cannot do, noble respect Takes it in might, not merit.' (The sentence is one of those anticipatory hints by which Shakespeare prepares his audience to interpret what follows—and leaves a clue to his actors of how to play the scene.) Demetrius, particularly, with the incisive tongue of Burbage, is more aggressively critical than his lord. The contrast is marked right from the start, when Theseus mildly wonders **if the Lion be to speak**, and provokes Demetrius's consciously smart riposte: **No wonder, my Lord: one Lion may, when many Asses do.**

[157-209] And so the play begins. We have already been prepared, by the committee in the wood, for the over-worked convention of the explanatory prologue: it is one of the main targets of Shakespeare's satire. Quince has provided us with three such prologues, his own, Wall's and Lion's—nay, three and a half, for Moonshine embarks upon a fourth before he is put out of countenance by garrulous heckling. Snout's prologue is purely informative, delivered with a matter-of-factness of manner and a trustfully confidential tone as of one letting his hearers into an important secret: the absence of any attempt at decorative ornament in the diction is in itself a comic effect, for it is contrasted with the audibly artificial measure of the versification:

> **This loam, this rough-cast, and this stone doth show,**
> **That I am that same Wall; the truth is so.**
> **And this the cranny is,**

(he will 'hold his fingers thus', as Bottom instructed him in the wood)

right and sinister,
Through which the fearful Lovers are to whisper.

The Duke's praise of Snout's performance is as genuine as it is deserved: **Would you desire Lime and Hair to speak better?** and he cuts short Demetrius's acid quip about **the wittiest partition**, to ensure silence for the entry of the heroic protagonist.

It is to be hoped that Will Kemp appreciated the brilliance of his colleague's verbal caricature, and that he did not obscure it by setting on some quantity of barren spectators to laugh at irrelevant antics and the stock stage-business of clowning. He had only to remember that Bottom the weaver was approaching his hour of opportunity and putting the last ounce of his histrionic genius into the great tragic role of Pyramus, 'that kills himself, most gallant, for love . . . let the audience look to their eyes'. Snout, perhaps, being absorbed in wide-eyed wonder at Bottom's virtuosity, is a little late in showing his **chink** and has to be nudged before he receives Pyramus's **Thanks**; and his reactions, at first of coy complacency to the flattery of **O sweet, O lovely wall**, and then of hurt astonishment to the abrupt volte-face of the disappointed lover, **Curst be thy stones for thus deceiving me**, are comical deviations from the tragic intensity of Quince's text. But it is the text itself, and his players' dedicated delivery of it, which provoke the continuous and contented laughter of the whole playhouse. It is true that some of the echoes, the literary allusions, parodies of the written word, make their full impact upon a limited section only of the audience; but the dramatic allusions, the recollection of previous performances (in this and other playhouses) of plays on the Pyramus-theme or other classical subjects, and of an earlier style of acting, will be obvious enough even to the injudicious, who have often applauded such rhetorical bombast and perhaps are still ready to enjoy it in the neighbouring playhouses where the tradition has not yet become outmoded.[25] Bottom, of course, is quite unaware of the inadequacy of Quince's text: Quince, though he aspires to heroic eloquence, is incapable of sustaining it. When the quick-witted, highly articulate Falstaff gives his imitation of 'King Cambises' vein', we have the well-turned splendour (absurd only because it is addressed to Mistress Quickly) of 'For God's sake Lords, convey my tristful Queen, For tears do stop the flood-gates of her eyes' (a couplet which an absent-minded examination candidate might place in the context of RICHARD II). Quince cannot rise to this level, and Bottom's orotund delivery is left stranded on a desolate shore of empty, resourceless truism and repetition:

> O grim look'd night, O night with hue so black,
> O night, which ever art, when day is not:
> O night, O night, alack, alack, alack . . .

The violence of his cursing of the **wicked wall, through whom** he sees **no bliss**, provokes the Duke's quizzical support of the offended victim: **The wall methinks being sensible** (it is certainly an animate wall; furthermore, Snout has—and shows—his feelings), **should curse again.** Whereupon Kemp breaks out of the character of Pyramus, but remains firmly anchored in the personality of Bottom: nothing could be more typical of him as we have grown to know him than his enthusiastic desire to put his highness right: **No in truth sir, he should not. 'Deceiving me' is Thisbe's cue; she is to enter now, and I am to spy her through the wall. You shall see it will fall pat as I told you; yonder she comes.** And he slips back into his part, awaiting his next cue. He is not word-perfect, but having made one slip, **I see a voice**, he sets the record straight by compensation:

> now will I to the chink,
> To spy an I can hear my Thisbe's face.

Shakespeare, in his handling of the burlesque lovers and their language, gently challenges his audience to remember his own lyrical treatment of the agonies of crossed love earlier in this play; the comic resemblance is more striking still to ROMEO AND JULIET, with its lovers, its parental intransigence, its divisive wall, its hero who kills himself upon a misunderstanding, and its heroine who devotedly follows his example.

The dalliance through the chink is given comic point by the device of rhyming stichomythia, by the mishandling of the famous names of Leander and Cephalus, by the choice of **Helen** (instead of Leander's chaste Hero) as a pattern of trustiness, perhaps by the sibilance of Flute's **Shafalus** which gives Bottom a moist earful, and the difficulty of negotiating a kiss **through the hole of this vile wall**. Certainly the blunder of **Ninny's tomb** does not go uncensured by the frustrated author: a growl of 'Ninus' tomb, man' is audible at least to the mind's ear. The lovers retire to opposite corners of the Study-space, and the end of 'Scene One' is marked by Wall's summary: in the same vein of downright statement as his previous speech, it seems to derive from the personality of Snout:

> **Thus have I, Wall, my part discharged so;**
> **And being done, thus Wall away doth go.**

Quince, perhaps, studies the mannerisms of his actors in composing his play, just as Shakespeare himself does.

[210-222]   During the brief intermission before the play is resumed, there is an exchange between the Duke and the Duchess of considerable importance in Shakespeare's overall plan. (It is moreover part of the material which Dover Wilson ascribes to a final revision in 1598.) Rising from his seat, to stretch his legs and warm his hands at the fire, he hears the aggressively intolerant criticism of his Amazon bride: **This is the silliest stuff that ever I heard**. He turns to face her, and the playhouse, and offers a mild corrective of this philistine attitude: **The best in this kind are but shadows, and the worst are no worse, if imagination amend them**. So often, when he speaks within the ambience of the playhouse, Shakespeare is especially impressive: the judicious among his audience will take the point, and agree with the truth of Hippolyta's rather grudging retort: **It must be your imagination then, and not theirs**. Her words are double-edged and cut both ways: hers is the kind of imagination that is incapable of amending the players. Her lord's reply is ambivalent too: **If we imagine no worse of them than they of themselves, they may pass for excellent men**. He pokes fun at the pretensions of the players (especially, no doubt, of Bottom), but at the same time he (or his creator, Shakespeare) gives a hint to the audience of the best way to get their money's worth from their visit to the playhouse; it is a plea for 'that willing suspension of disbelief for the moment, which constitutes poetic faith'. Theseus is Shakespeare's ideal patron of the arts.

[222-313] **Here come two noble beasts in, a man and a Lion**. Snug the joiner, who is 'slow of study', and who was told sharply by Quince that he can do the Lion's part 'extempore, for it is nothing but roaring', has a speaking part after all: moreover we have seen him being put through the first paces of his prologue by Bottom in the wood—'Ladies, or fair Ladies, I would wish you, or I would request you. . . .' Now, speaking through the lion's neck, he addresses himself with most civil consideration to the ladies

> **. . . whose gentle hearts do fear**
> **The smallest monstrous mouse that creeps on floor . . .**

and tries for the moment to make them quake and tremble as he rolls his 'r'-sounds and growls his way through the alliteration of

> **When Lion rough in wildest rage doth roar.**

A change of rhyme-scheme (pairs instead of alternation) marks an engaging change of demeanour:

> **Then know that I, as Snug the Joiner am**
> **A Lion fell, nor else no Lion's dam . . .**

and he, like the Wall before him, earns his commendation of the Duke as **a very gentle beast, and of a good conscience**. Snug, being slow of study, can make nothing of the courtiers' chop-logic that follows, and retires baffled to make way for Starveling. As the interlude moves from absurdity to absurdity, the Duke himself begins to join in the mockery; but it is he who calls a halt to the banter: **It is well; leave it to his discretion, and let us listen to the Moon**. But Starveling does not get a fair hearing: like Holofernes before him, he is 'put out of countenance' by the relentless rivalry of wit in which the Duke too cannot resist competing. Twice the old man attempts to deliver the speech which he has taken great pains to con by heart:

> **This lanthorn doth the horned Moon present:**
> **My self, the man i'th'Moon do seem to be.**

But his hecklers are implacable, and even Hippolyta finds a jest to join in the baiting: **I am aweary of this Moon; would he would change.** Once again we notice that it is Theseus who, rebuking himself and his courtiers, secures him a hearing: **in courtesy, in all reason, we must stay the time.** Granted his audience at last, Starveling, with a touch of wholly pardonable asperity, speaks his mind in his own person (and appropriately in a rush of prose): **All that I have to say, is to tell you, that the Lanthorn is the Moon; I, the man i'th'Moon; this thorn bush, my thorn bush; and this dog, my dog.** The climax, focused upon the bland indifference of the dog's demeanour, raises a roar of laughter throughout the playhouse. And Starveling, as uncomprehending of the joke as the dog himself, with statuesque dignity takes up a central position as presiding genius over the scene that follows. Shakespeare's Moon, pervasive presence in the long night in the woods, was created, we remember, by other means. **But silence, here comes Thisbe.**

Flute scampers in—and immediately sets poor Quince's teeth on edge with the incorrigible solecism of **old Ninny's tomb.** The complicated manoeuvres of the sequel are all reflected in the exhortations of the court: they need no elaboration:

> **Well roar'd Lion.**
> **Well run Thisbe.**
> **Well shone Moon . . .**
> **Well mous'd Lion.**
> **And then came Pyramus.**
> **And so the Lion vanish'd.**

When Pyramus takes the stage, the Moon continues to shine **with a good grace**, and Bottom, thanking him in an audacious paradox, launches into the lavish alliterations and apostrophes of Quince's rhetoric. The even flow of pentameters is abruptly broken by a startling change of metre (unrecognised in the lineation of the early texts):

> **But stay: O spite!**
> **But mark, poor Knight,**
> **What dreadful dole is here?**
> **Eyes do you see!**
> **How can it be!**
> **O dainty Duck: O Dear!**

Bottom is determined to 'condole in some measure'. Unconscious of bathos and the absurdity of the alliterative device (**Quail, crush, conclude, and quell**) and cliché (the appeal to the Fates, the indignant questioning of the natural order—**O wherefore, Nature, didst thou Lions frame?**), he presses on to the grand climax of his suicide: drawing his sword, locating (with some hesitation) **that left pap, where heart doth hop**, he stabs himself four times (**Thus die I, thus, thus, thus**) and sinks to the floor. But in a moment he is sitting up again, to tell us:

> **Now am I dead,**
> **Now am I fled,**
> **My soul is in the sky.**[26]

It may be that the cadence is a little marred by Starveling's failure to co-operate: both old and deaf, he has lost touch with his surroundings and, during Bottom's great monologues, is falling asleep on his feet. Pyramus must ask a second time:

> **Moon take thy flight . . .**

With Starveling's departure, Bottom is left free to die in earnest: and he makes the most of every syllable of death:

Now die, die, die, die, die.

Perhaps Shakespeare asked his quartet of lovers to join Pyramus in
the last beat of his dramatic count-down.

[314-355]   The barrage of wise-cracks which greets the death of
Pyramus is the Chamberlain's Men's mirror-image of the kind of
reception they may sometimes have suffered in the Great Chamber of
some nobleman's house. But there is a shrewd stroke of dramatic
irony in the Duke's suggestion that the dead man **might yet recover,
and prove an Ass.** Kemp surely raised his head from the floor to cast
a suspicious glance at the speaker. Hippolyta, a stickler for realism, is
put out because **Moon-shine is gone before Thisbe comes back,
and finds her Lover.** But Theseus smilingly brushes aside her objection, rationalising the deficiency of Quince's scrip: **She will find him
by star-light.** And for the last time he asks for the attention of the
audience: **Here she comes, and her passion ends the play.** We can
deduce, from the prolonged commentary of the talkative courtiers,
Flute's elaborate by-play of searching for her lover by star-light until
Lysander observes that **she hath spied him already, with those
sweet eyes.**

Flute, for his final aria, has made quite sure of metre and rhyme:
yet the rapid phrases of dramatic discovery are difficult to present
within the strict formality of his author's versification, and he has not
solved the problem:

> **Asleep my Love?**
> **What, dead my Dove?**
> **O Pyramus arise:**
> **Speak, Speak. Quite dumb?**
> **Dead, dead? A tomb**
> **Must cover thy sweet eyes.**

But for all the absurdity of the itemised description of her dead lover—
the **Lily Lips**, the **cherry nose**, and the rest—not for one moment
does Thisbe relax the intensity of her lament. The general appeal of
Lovers make moan receives immediate particular response from the

pairs of lovers that are her audience. Expository gestures illustrate the cruel action of the Fates in severing **with shears, his thread of silk.** Inevitably the **trusty sword** is hard to find, for it is buried beneath her lover's body, and must perhaps be offered to her by his own dead hand. When its blade has imbrued her breast, she addresses her farewells to each of the three wedded couples in turn: **Adieu, adieu, adieu.** It is a bravura performance, and is greeted with hearty applause on stage, taken up by the whole playhouse, Galleries, Yard and all. And the lamentable comedy is over.

[356-379] Not quite, though: for while the Duke is counting the survivors (**Moon-shine and Lion are left to bury the dead**) and Demetrius remembers the **Wall too**, the irrepressible Bottom rises from the dead, to correct error: **No, I assure you, the wall is down, that parted their Fathers.** Displacing Flute, who lies heavy on his chest, he struggles to his feet, to ask if the Duke would care **to see the Epilogue, or to hear a Bergamask dance, between two of our company.** The Duke, with great good-humour, side-steps the Epilogue (**your play needs no excuse**) and, permitting himself a quip at the expense of the author (**Marry, if he that writ it had played Pyramus, and hang'd himself in Thisbe's garter, it would have been a fine Tragedy**), then graciously comforts the disconsolate Quince with a tactful compliment: **and so it is truly, and very notably discharged.** And so, letting the Epilogue alone at the Duke's request, they settle for the Bergamask dance. We remember* that Bottom decided upon a Ballett to recount his dream and to be sung 'at her death'. The Bergamask is not far from his original intention, although, since no words survive, we cannot know whether or not it was danced to vocal music. But whatever the accompaniment, Bottom has devised a dance to illustrate his 'most rare vision'—a dance to be executed by 'two of our company', himself, wearing a buckram Asshead, and Flute, robed still for Thisbe, but with a paper crown above his flowing wig remembering Titania. The dance ends the interlude of the mechanicals, and Philostrate, in ushering them out of the palace, presents to Quince the Duke's largesse to the company—if not sixpence a day, at least a welcome remuneration for their pains.

* See *note* 20.

During the Bergamask, a bell in the Tiring-House has begun to strike the hour, and by the time the mechanicals have departed, the Duke can hear the last stroke sounding:

The iron tongue of midnight hath told twelve.
Lovers to bed, 'tis almost Fairy time.

Theseus, who 'never may believe . . . these Fairy toys', speaks, of course, with a sceptic's irony. The 'long age of three hours, Between our after supper, and bed-time' has been well beguiled by **this palpable gross play**. The illusion of passing time is a commonplace in all drama, but especially potent with the spell-binding aid of poetry. **Sweet friends to bed**. The Duke's concluding couplet, suggesting the familiar milieu of the festival season at Whitehall or Hampton Court—

A fortnight hold we this solemnity,
In nightly Revels, and new jollity

—has all the appearance of finality. Music, we may guess, accompanies a ceremonial departure of each couple in turn, the Duke and the Duchess appearing perhaps for a moment in the Chamber above, with servants conducting them by candlelight to bed. The façade of the Tiring-House has acquired greater definition as part of the ducal palace: the Stage where the interlude was played is the Great Hall, the Chamber is the familiar Gallery overlooking it. Our play is done.

[V.ii.1-53] And yet it is not. Here is another of Shakespeare's tricks of bluff. Although some editors, perhaps reflecting the practice of the scenery theatre, mark at this moment the opening of a new scene, in Shakespeare's playhouse the continuity is unbroken and the sequel immediate: this continuity conveys a charming irony, as the Duke's scepticism recoils upon itself. It is, after all, fairy time. And though we have forgotten them, the surprise of the fairies' returning is all the more delightful because we should have been expecting them: Oberon promised (and we have just heard from the Duke an echo of his phrases) that they would 'tomorrow midnight, solemnly Dance in Duke Theseus' house triumphantly, And bless it to all fair prosperity'. And here they come; Puck first, springing up (through the Trap-Door) from among the embers of the fire. He carries a branch of broom. With 'the iron tongue of midnight' night and darkness have begun to creep back into the daylit theatre. Now Puck's words, with their imagery of snoring sleeper and wasted brands and churchyards, take the evocation a step farther: we feel powerfully that the palace is asleep. Moreover he is out to curdle our blood a little—or so it seems from his opening lines:

> **Now the hungry Lion roars**
> **And the Wolf behowls the Moon . . .**

The sound of **behowls**[27] imitates the sense, and it is echoed in the diphthongs of **screech-owl, screeching loud,** and the rhyme that rounds off the uneasy midnight insomnia of **the wretch that lies in woe**, whom the bird of omen puts

> **In remembrance of a shroud.**

What is the goblin up to? The goblin who is 'fear'd in field and town'? Relentlessly he pursues his spine-chilling theme:

> **Now it is the time of night,**
> **That the graves, all gaping wide,**
> **Every one lets forth his sprite,**
> **In the Church-way paths to glide.**

This is no epithalamion. Long, long ago, it seems, the Duke opened the play with the command to 'turn melancholy forth to Funerals: The pale companion is not for our pomp'. It is at first puzzling that Shakespeare should allow Puck to strike this jarring note in the midst of his wedding-festivities. His purpose becomes clear in the sequel. Oberon and Titania are coming to bless the bridal house, to ward off the dangers that lie in wait for the newly-wed in their nuptial hour. The poet therefore dramatises the dangers first, so that the benign protection of the fairies may seem the more necessary and the more effective. This is the purpose of Puck's grisly speech: a late stanza of Spenser's *Epithalamion* puts his evocation of terror into perspective:

> Let no lamenting cryes, nor dolefull teares,
> Be heard all night within nor yet without:
> Ne let false whispers, breeding hidden feares,
> Breake gentle sleepe with misconceived dout.
> Let no deluding dreames, nor dreadful sights
> Make sudden sad affrights;
> Ne let housefyres, nor lightnings helpeless harmes,
> Ne let the Pouke, nor other evill sprights,
> Ne let mischivous witches with theyr charmes,
> Ne let hob Goblins, names whose sence we see not,
> Fray us with things that be not.
> Let not the shriech Oule, nor the Storke be heard:
> Nor the night Raven that still deadly yels,
> Nor damned ghosts cald up with mighty spels,
> Nor griesly vultures make us once affeard:
> Ne let th'unpleasant Quyre of Frogs still croking
> Make us to wish theyr choking.
> Let none of these theyr drery accents sing;
> Ne let the woods them answer, nor theyr eccho ring.

The modulation from terror to comfort is smoothly and ingeniously handled: as from every available entry—poking a head round each of the two Doors, peering inquisitively into the Study—one by one into the unfamiliar terrain of a ducal palace come our old acquaintance, Peaseblossom and Cobweb and Moth and Mustardseed and the rest, Puck's verse takes on a new, less sinister tone:

> **And we Fairies, that do run,**
> **By the triple Hecate's team,**
> **From the presence of the Sun,**
> **Following darkness like a dream,**
> **Now are frolic . . .**

The word itself—**frolic**—has an abrupt brightness which dispels the gloom; and the ensuing gear-change (slipping into a couplet-rhyme) completes the transformation:

> **not a Mouse**
> **Shall disturb this hallowed house.**

Then with his sprig of broom he sweeps **the dust behind the door**, to prepare a way for the entry of the King and Queen. Broom and candle were traditional attributes of Robin Goodfellow.

The King, continuing Puck's evocation of the sleeping palace, at once prescribes the ensuing ritual:

> **Through the house give glimmering light,**
> **By the dead and drowsy fire . . .**

Each of the fairies in turn lights his taper (with the assistance of the back-stage men below the Trap-Door) at the embers of the dying fire. Their instructions are

> **. . . this Ditty after me,**
> **Sing and dance it trippingly.**

The Queen adds her commands:

> **First rehearse your song by rote,**
> **To each word a warbling note.**
> **Hand in hand with Fairy grace,**
> **Will we sing and bless this place.**

Then the ceremony begins. There seems little doubt how the lines of the text we have were distributed:[28] Oberon sings the first two lines: their imperative content makes this clear:

> **Now until the break of day,**
> **Through this house each Fairy stray.**

Then all the fairies, singing 'after' their King, chant in chorus:

> **To the best Bride-bed will we,**
> **Which by us shall blessed be . . .**

and the purpose of their choric song is apotropaeic, to ward off all **the blots of Nature's hand** from the issue of **the couples three**:

> **Never mole, harelip, nor scar,**
> **Nor mark prodigious, such as are**
> **Despised in Nativity,**
> **Shall upon their children be.**

There the song ends, and Oberon speaks the rest. During the song, Puck presents 'field dew' to the King and Queen, who dance majestically round the hearth, sprinkling the Stage and making gestures of ceremonial purification. At the close of the song, Puck carries the 'field dew' to each of the fairies in turn, while Oberon gives them explicit instructions:

> **With this field dew consecrate,**
> **Every Fairy take his gait,**
> **And each several chamber bless,**
> **Through this Palace with sweet peace;**
> **And the owner of it bless'd**
> **Ever shall in safety rest.**

It is a restful cadence, a full close of perfect concord, rallentando and pause. Then he revives the tempo for a busy, purposeful departure (throwing in an intermediate rhyme to break the solemn mood):

> **Trip away, make no stay;**
> **Meet me all by break of day.**

And the fairies, holding their tapers aloft (or wearing them on their heads)* and shaking field dew from the fingers of the other hand, depart hither and thither to set about the business of the night. The

* See *page* 117, *above.*

King and Queen, perhaps, are seen for a moment aloft in the Chamber, seeking their way 'to the best Bride-bed', following in the steps of the Duke and Duchess. And for the second time the play, it seems, is done.

[54-69]   But Shakespeare has one more trick to play on us. Puck has disappeared into the embers of the dead and drowsy fire. Now he bounces out of the Trap-Door once again: and this time he is not only Puck, but confessedly an actor (a 'shadow') and the poet's mouth-piece, and he speaks directly to the playhouse audience: and as he speaks, he sets echoes of past moments in the play ringing in our ears:

> **If we shadows have offended,**

(the best in this kind are but shadows)

> **Think but this (and all is mended)**
> **That you have but slumb'red here,**
> **While these visions did appear.**

(all this derision Shall seem a dream, and fruitless vision)

> **And this weak and idle theme,**
> **No more yielding but a dream,**

(think no more of this night's accidents, But as the fierce vexation of a dream)

> **Gentles, do not reprehend.**
> **If you pardon, we will mend.**

With unabashed charm, he pleads that he and his fellow-actors may escape the hissing of **the Serpent's tongue**, and makes irresistible appeal to the goodwill of the audience:

> **Give me your hands, if we be friends.**

The whole playhouse, we may be sure, took the hint. The transition from the world of the imagination to prosaic reality must always be made at the end of a play: Shakespeare and his company liked to make it easier for their audience to readjust themselves. Some such reason prompted the custom of dancing a jig after a tragedy. Even Prospero in later years will beg the indulgence of his audience. Some such reason is the justification of Puck's humdrum apology. But it is not wholly perfunctory: it reminds us that the play's title promised us a Dream: it reminds us too that Hippolyta hoped to dream away the time before her marriage, and that the lovers remember their adventures only as a vision. All the characters in the play, since they are actors, are shadows, but Puck and his fellow-fairies as creatures of darkness are shadows of another kind (believe me, King of shadows, I mistook): it is as an actor that he apologises to his audience, but it is as Robin Goodfellow that he promises to **restore amends**. Like Prospero, he plays delicately with his audience's disbelief. After the spell cast by the fairies' benediction, we are back with our neighbours in the Yard or the Galleries of the playhouse, and must struggle home through the drab streets or across the river in the London afternoon. Robin's restoration of amends is itself a kind of benediction.

NOTES

Page 35
1 The thematic and verbal affinities of the play, the overtones both literary and theatrical, are fully explored and discussed in the first chapter ('Backgrounds') of David P. Young's *Something of Great Constancy*. See also Kenneth Muir, *Shakespeare's Sources*, vol. I, 31 ff.

Page 36
2 It is possible, but unlikely, that 'Stand forth Demetrius' and 'Stand forth Lysander' are stage-directions to the actors. Both Quarto and Folio print them so, and Rowe was the first editor to suggest the now accepted interpretation of the phrases as part of the dialogue: it would seem an improbable coincidence that both phrases, mere stage-directions, nevertheless make a complete pentameter with the following words.

Page 39
3 A typical example of such an opinion is that of Dover Wilson, *New Cambridge* edition, 91 f.: 'Few readers of the play will dispute that, if *A Midsummer Night's Dream* be a text composed at different periods, the episodes concerning the lovers, episodes wherein the psychology is generally as crude as the verse is stiff and antithetical, are likely to belong to the earliest stratum.' For an antidote to this opinion see Young, 68 f.

Page 40
4 'Lysander describes in little the sort of tragedy presented in *Romeo and Juliet*, where Juliet exclaimed that their love was "Too like the lightning, which doth cease to be Ere one can say 'it lightens' " (II.ii.119–120).' C. L. Barber, *Shakespeare's Festive Comedy*, 126.

Page 49
5 Young, 34 ff., examines the dramatic antecedents of 'Ercles' vein' and argues that it 'reflects the worst aspects of the popular drama of the 1570s and

80s'. It was not long since the stage had been held by 'A lamentable tragedye, mixed full of plesant mirth, containing the life of Cambises, king of Persia'. And the fashion was by no means wholly dead.

Page 50

6 Glynne Wickham, *Early English Stages 1300 to 1660*, vol. II, Part II, 183, considers the functions of the book-keeper, who 'became responsible for back-stage discipline' and acted as 'the prompter-producer in rehearsal and performance'. He continues by noting 'that Shakespeare entrusts these duties in *A Midsummer Night's Dream* to Peter Quince who, by trade, is said to be a carpenter. Amateur and artisan as the players of *Pyramus and Thisbe* undoubtedly are, may we infer that the portrait of this patient and resourceful stage-manager gently satirizes that other carpenter-turned-actor, James Burbage, father to Richard and Cuthbert, builder of the Theater, and purchaser of the Blackfriars, who was so familiar a figure both to the actors of the play and to the audiences of the time? Another person whose background was similarly compounded of carpentry and theatrical pretensions was Inigo Jones; a fact that gave Ben Jonson an equal opportunity for satirical portraiture and one that he exploited with a less gentle pen than Shakespeare's.'

Page 52

7 Young, 57: 'The fashion for presenting them [the fairies] had sprung from the entertainments presented for Elizabeth, and their first use in drama proper was probably in Lyly's *Endymion* (1588). However, Greene had already used them in *James the Fourth*, where Oberon himself brings them on to dance. Oberon also was probably familiar to the popular audiences from a dramatization of *Huon of Bordeaux*.'

8 M. W. Latham in *The Elizabethan Fairies* has investigated the relationship between Shakespeare's fairies and the fairies of folk tradition. Her general conclusion is that, while Shakespeare incorporated many details of living popular belief, much of his conception is original. Certainly his treatment of the fairy-world, at its most extensive in A MIDSUMMER NIGHT's DREAM, profoundly influenced poets and dramatists, and, when his careful balance between poetic fantasy and an older, earthier reality degenerated in the hands of more sentimental writers, eventually provided the substance of later popular traditon.

Page 55

9 Latham, 187 ff., shows that the diminutive size of the fairies, so essential a feature of the later tradition, was probably not a part of the native belief of Shakespeare's own day, but largely his own invention.

10 Latham, 219 ff., argues that Puck, Robin Goodfellow or Hobgoblin was 'not a native of fairyland'. He sprang from a different tradition, more devilish than fairy-like; and 'of all the spirits who were believed to haunt England, there was not one whom [Shakespeare] could have better chosen to give a sense of reality to his fairy plot, or to furnish, to an audience, the immediate assurance of boisterous gayety and of harmless fun'.

Page 57
11 Latham, 182, implies that Shakespeare deliberately invented this unusual provenance for his fairies. The Folio and the Roberts Quarto have the reading 'steepe': the Fisher Quarto has 'steppe'.

Page 72
12 If there were indeed, as we have suggested, rushes upon the Stage, they would have given visible substance to Quince's phrase 'This green plot shall be our stage'. They are appropriate too as rushes in the presence strewed when in the last Act the Stage represents the ducal palace. Rushes with their evocative smell would seem to have fitted the Athenian wood better than the green baize which, according to Law's suggestion (quoted by Kermode in the *Arden* edition of THE TEMPEST, 153), may have been used in court performance to represent the 'grass-plot' of that play.

Page 75
13 The suggestion comes from Young, 42: he has an interesting paragraph on 'the parallels . . . between the mechanicals' attempts at drama and the older plays that Shakespeare and his audiences felt they had outgrown'.

Page 77
14 Young's discussion of 'Backgrounds' has already been recommended to the reader. Analysing the affinities and precedents which would strike 'the full range of the cross section' of the public audience, he pinpoints the allusive comedy which underlies the direct appeal of the moment when Titania wakes. The humour rises, he argues, from the unfamiliar juxtaposition of familiar elements: 'As Bottom meets Titania . . . the popular stage joins hands with the world of court entertainment; folklore is introduced to myth; grossness chats

with refinement; bestiality dallies with spirituality. . . . *A Midsummer Night's Dream* is a remarkable synthesis of comic materials, a courtly comedy with enough appeal for the popular stage' (Young, 15).

Page 81
15 Another example of Shakespeare's use of the device of reconstructive narration is Benvolio's account of the death of Mercutio and Tybalt, ROMEO AND JULIET, III.i.158 ff. Among later examples a striking instance is Iago's narration of Cassio's drunken brawling, OTHELLO, II.iii.222 ff., where the villain disguises his malicious intent by appearing to 'mince this matter, Making it light to Cassio'.

Page 102
16 See Dover Wilson's *New Cambridge* edition of the play, 158, and, on the question of candles in the private theatre, Irwin Smith, *Shakespeare's Black-friars Playhouse*, 301 f.

Page 107
17 Dover Wilson, 158, comments on *Sleepers Lye still*: 'This last was a very necessary addition, seeing that the sleepers are to "start up" at the sound of horns after l.137 and might therefore easily mistake the horns which announce Theseus at l.101 for their cue unless great care was observed.'

Page 108
18 The hint for the hunting-scene may well have come from Chaucer, *The Knight's Tale*, 815–824. Chaucer's Theseus is so much the huntsman that at the dawn of every day in the month of May he is dressed and ready to ride out 'with hunte and horne and houndes hym bisyde'. The picture of Theseus the huntsman seems to have become traditional. It is interesting that Chaucer uses the device of the May-time hunt for exactly the same purpose as Shakespeare. His Theseus too must be drawn out into the wood near Athens where by inevitable coincidence the rival lovers, Palamon and Arcite, are.

Page 109
19 In *The Knight's Tale* the same device of May-day observance precipitates a coincidental gathering of different characters in the woods. The reader who wishes to taste the full flavour of the May-day associations should look at the famous illustration portraying the month of May in *Les Très Riches Heures du Duc de Berry*; although not of Shakespeare's period, it conveys perfectly the

mood of gaiety in man and nature. Young, 16 ff., examines the 'ambience of festivity' Shakespeare created by associating his play 'with three kinds of celebration—royal marriage and the May and Midsummer holidays'.

Page 112

20 In all the early texts Bottom uses the word 'ballet' to describe Quince's projected setting of *Bottom's Dream*. Most editors substitute 'ballad' without comment; this is not unreasonable: to Shakespeare's contemporaries the words seem to have been interchangeable. In the Folio text of THE WINTER'S TALE (IV.iii.261 ff.) the Clown asks Autolycus 'What hast heere? Ballads?' and the ingenuous Mopsa chimes in, 'Pray now buy some: I love a ballet in print . . . for then we are sure they are true.' But to a modern reader the simple substitution of one word for the other is a little misleading. We are apt today to associate the word 'ballad' with the particular sense of 'a simple spirited poem in short stanzas . . . in which some popular story is graphically narrated' (*O.E.D.*), and this sense was not current in the time of Shakespeare. Another sense, 'a popular song . . . celebrating or scurrilously attacking persons or institutions', was indeed current in Shakespeare's time—and this is the ballad of the broadsheets, the kind sold by Autolycus. But it seems probable that Bottom's 'ballet' is neither of these; he refers instead to the Elizabethan musical form known to modern scholars as a 'ballett' (and usually spelt thus). The ballett was a light-hearted song, usually strophic in form and with a nonsense refrain of 'fa la' or the like, and often used for dancing. Thomas Morley in his *A Plain and Easy Introduction to Practical Music* of 1597 (in R. Alec Harman's modern edition, 295) summarises the current forms of 'music for voices'; after dealing with 'the grave ditties', he moves on to 'the light music' which 'hath been of late more deeply dived into so that there is no vanity which in it hath not been followed to the full'. Among the lightest forms, he says, are the 'country songs' which serve 'to make a clownish music to a clownish matter'; but, he continues, 'there is also another kind more light than this which they term Balletti or dances, and are songs which being sung to a ditty may likewise be danced. . . . There be also another kind of Balletts commonly called "Fa las" . . . a slight kind of music it is and, as I take it, devised to be danced to voices.' It is either Morley's balletts (with 'fa las') or his balletti (without) that Quince is to emulate: in either case *Bottom's Dream* is to be danced as well as sung. In the event the mechanicals offer the Duke a 'Bergamask dance', a clownish peasant dance, often, like the ballett, with vocal music. On this form too Morley has a word to say: 'There is likewise a kind of songs (which I had almost forgotten) called Giustinianas and are all written in the Bergamasca language; a wanton and rude kind of music it is, and like enough to carry the name of some notable courtesan of the city of Bergamo. . . .'

Page 117

21 Dover Wilson, 98, says: 'It would almost seem . . . as if the success of the fairy-masque at the original private performance of *A Midsummer Night's Dream* persuaded Shakespeare's company to introduce the same device, or rather an inferior imitation of it, into their hastily written and scantily rehearsed version of *The Merry Wives of Windsor* for the Court.'

22 The lineation of Theseus's speech is clearly faulty in all the early texts; in our reconstruction we have followed the regular version favoured by all editors. The reader is referred to Dover Wilson's analysis of the faulty lineation and the conclusions about the transmission of the text which he draws from it (*New Cambridge* edition, 80 ff.).

Page 119

23 R. G. White writes: 'Would Shakespeare, after thus reaching the climax of his thought, fall a-twaddling about bushes and bears? Note too the loss of dignity in the rhythm. I cannot even bring myself to doubt that these lines are interpolated.' In the process of preserving Shakespeare's dignity, how often we forget that he was a player-playwright making plays for players!

Page 123

24 If Dover Wilson's account of the textual history of the play is correct, in the earlier draft Philostrate paves the way for an unvaried barrage of banter in the sequel. It is only in a later revision that we can perceive this delicate transition of mood in Theseus by which in the end his repeated determination to hear the interlude springs from the humane motives of an enlightened patron.

Page 129

25 'The scenes of grief and death in "Pyramus and Thisby" are, in fact, a systematic mockery of similar moments in older plays', Young, 38. He points out that 'Shakespeare's rival theater was still presenting plays in the Senecan style if not in Cambises' vein. It was still possible in 1614, if we are to believe the prologue to *Bartholomew Fair*, to find those "who swear *Ieronimo* and *Andronicus* are the best plays yet".' The *literary* 'sources' of Quince's 'Pyramus and Thisbe' are given in full in Muir, 31 ff.

Page 134

26 The superfluous information of his own death given us by Pyramus derives from the precedent of Cambises himself (Young, 38). It seems that Shakespeare was conscious of the danger (in the hands of less competent craftsmen) of a convention he himself followed; he quickly outgrew the cruder formulas of the tragic convention, as we can see if we compare Richard II's 'Mount, mount my soul' with Antony's death in silence or Lear's in incoherence. Yet the testimony to Shakespeare's skill as a parodist is that the devices of dialogue used to comic effect in 'Pyramus and Thisbe' may be seen again in some of the most serious moments of the poet's own work. Hamlet himself seems to follow Cambises's precedent with 'I am dead Horatio . . . Horatio, I am dead . . . O I die, Horatio. . . . ' The grief of Pyramus is expressed in a comic change of tense ('. . . which is: no, no, which was the fairest Dame That liv'd . . .'), and the same device is used to moving effect in JULIUS CAESAR: 'Is not that he?—No, this was he Messala, But Cassius is no more.' Even the repetitive expansion of a line seems to appear in the Folio OTHELLO: 'Oh Desdemon! dead Desdemon: dead. Oh, oh!'

Page 138

27 The early texts read 'beholds'. The generally accepted emendation 'behowls' is almost certainly right. Cf. As YOU LIKE IT, V.ii.121.

Page 140

28 The distribution we have adopted is substantially that recommended by Richmond Noble. His reasoning and his discussion of the Folio direction will be found in *Shakespeare's Use of Song*, 55 ff.